Volume 2 ———————————————————————————— DENMARK

DENMARK

06
Masthead

07
Editor's Letter

72
Ingredient Glossary

138
Locations

144
Social

10
A Love Letter to Alain Passard
Frederik Bille Brahe

12
John Kofod Pedersen:
Sortebro Kro

20
The Pølse of a Nation
Jonathan Shipley

24
Nicolai Nørregaard:
Kadeau

36
René and Nadine Redzepi:
Noma

48
Christian Puglisi:
Relæ

60
Matthew Orlando:
Amass Restaurant

76
Schønnemann
Matt Duckor

78
Per Hallundbaek:
Falsled Kro

90
Rasmus Kofoed:
Geranium

98
Bo Bech:
Geist

106
Rocket Launch
Matt Duckor

108
Rosio Sánchez:
Hija de Sánchez

118
Frederik Bille Brahe:
Atelier September

132
Blocks
Mads Refslund

134
Overthrowing the Dictators
Bo Bech

ADAM GOLDBERG
Editor in Chief

DANIELA VELASCO
Creative Director

ELYSSA GOLDBERG
Executive Editor

BONJWING LEE
Copy Editor

CONTRIBUTORS
Bo Bech
Charlotte Dupont
Erika Velasco
Frederik Bille Brahe
Jonathan Shipley
Mads Refslund
Matt Duckor

WELCOME

The first time I visited Noma, I was presented with a large white plate piled high with raw beef and a mound of bright, lemony sorrel. There were no forks and knives; we were instead encouraged to use a pinch-and-swipe technique to shuttle the tartare into our mouths. The dish seemed simple enough—maybe something I would try to recreate at home.

But then I asked about the ingredients. The tartare was flanked by a dehydrated juniper berry powder on one side and a tarragon emulsion on the other. The wood sorrel was picked that same day from a neighboring municipal park. (On a subsequent visit, I learned its origin firsthand when René Redzepi sent me to the park to forage it before the meal.)

A later variation of the dish replaced lemony herbs with ants—their formic acid providing the burst of brightness on which the plate previously relied.

The intense dedication to experimentation, honing technique, always doing more while seemingly presenting less, and showcasing ingredients that are exclusively Danish, is what makes Noma one of the most influential restaurants in the world. It has become an incubator for a generation of young chefs whose restaurants continue to push those boundaries. Except, now, many are beginning to rebel against the words that came to define Noma's New Nordic era—hyperlocal, seasonal, and foraged—to pave their own way.

What does that rebellion look like? And what is next for Denmark 12 years after Noma disrupted dining?

Using the New Nordic movement as a waypoint, *Ambrosia*, Volume 2: Denmark traces the evolution of Danish cooking through three periods: before, during, and after. We follow the trail from traditional pickled herring to Mexican tacos, from five-ingredient recipes you can make for dinner tonight to others that will leave you awe-struck by their obscurity and intricacy.

ADAM GOLDBERG, Editor in Chief

A Love Letter to Alain Passard
By Frederik Bille Brahe

It was a cold March day in Paris when I had my first meal at L'Arpège. The tables weren't numbered; they were labeled as different herbs. I sat at "Angelique," a corner table near the kitchen. I had dreamed of eating there since I started cooking as a kid. I was with my parents; they had taken me there as a gift.

Years later, I return as often as I can to L'Arpège, usually alone and always at ease. I feel relaxed there. It's home. From my table, I can see Alain Passard preparing his vegetable couscous, a dish that he has poetically named *Jardinière Arlequin, semoule à l'huile d'argan*. I think I have had it at least 10 times over the last 10 years and, still, I'm amazed by the courage, simplicity, and perfection with which Alain cooks it. He serves me the dish as he always does, with his kind smile and tender attention.

I only speak a little French and he only speaks a little English, but we are like two young lovers looking at each other. Trying to communicate is often difficult, so we try instead to gaze deeply into each other's eyes, reassuring one another that we are content in each other's presence.

The couscous is amazing, of course—and the vegetarian merguez that accompanies it is too. I taste it—my eyes closed—and my heart fills with a deep sorrow, because I'm not the one who cooked it.

The first time I tried that dish was the moment I knew what I wanted to do in my own kitchen, should I ever be lucky enough to run one. That dream became real in 2012. Saison, the famous restaurant in Denmark where I worked as a sous chef, closed, leaving me a free agent. Even though Saison had a similar approach to cooking as L'Arpège, it was only when I decided to open a place of my own that I knew I wanted to commit to this philosophy wholeheartedly. I was thinking of what my restaurant should be, and I kept circling back to one idea: Alain Passard and his vegetables. I wanted to do in Copenhagen what he did in Paris.

I felt so strongly that this was what I should offer my guests—poetry and art expressed through gentle cooking—that

I moved quickly. I found a place in the city center—an amazing old antique store that I could convert into a restaurant. But the space was small, and it quickly became apparent that all I could get away with there was a small cafe of forty square meters, about 18 seats. I wouldn't be allowed to serve alcohol and I had to close at 6 pm.

But I pressed on, undeterred. I was so determined, maybe even stubborn, and the limitations didn't dissuade me. I was absolutely certain I could create something special in that space, that I could create the L'Arpège-like restaurant I wanted.

Atelier September Butik

ons - fredag kl. 12 - 17.30
Lørdag   kl.   11 - 16

Atelier September Cafe

Man - fredag   kl. 07.30 - 18.00
Lørdag   kl. 09.00 - 16.00
Søndag kl. 10.00 - 16.00

John Kofod Pedersen

SORTEBRO KRO, ODENSE
55.36685° N, 10.38387° E

There is no better place on earth to spend the Christmas holiday than at Sortebro Kro, the deeply traditional restaurant on Funen, a pastoral island in the middle of Denmark. The restaurant was built in Hans Christian Andersen's hometown of Odense in 1805, the same year the prolific author was born. Two centuries later, John Kofod, the chef at Sortebro Kro, is one of the nation's stars. He's been entrusted with thousands of years of Danish culinary history, including the classic, bountiful herring feasts for which the restaurant is famous. Even now—especially now—as his peers are redefining Danish cuisine, Kofod's Sorterbro Kro remains relevant and exciting. It holds to tradition, yet, through exquisite cooking and a constant process of refinement, makes the old seem new again.

How did you get started owning your own restaurant?

On a cold winter day in 1998, I was looking in the newspaper and saw that there was a restaurant for sale. I showed it to my wife, and told her I needed to see it because I had been there when I was a 13-year-old. I drove five hours from Copenhagen with my mother-in-law to see it. I remember it being very cold.

What kind of food did you serve there?

We were adamant about not making French or Italian food. We just called it The Kitchen of Taste. I don't even know how that started, but we still call it that. Thinking back, I think the food was half French cuisine and half Danish cuisine. At the time, we weren't proud of our own products, so we were importing cheese, duck—everything—from France. Today, we're almost only using Danish products.

How would you characterize your style of cooking?

We have a signature menu of eight courses and a tasting menu of 15 courses, and they are rooted in traditional Danish dishes, such as braised calf, rye bread, and fiskefilet. Everything on the menu changes every six weeks or so.

Does the pickled herring stay on the menu?

In Denmark, we are quite famous for our herring. You can't believe how much herring we serve at Sortebro Kro. We actually dedicate an entire week to just cutting and marinating them for Christmas. One of them is marinated with brown sugar and vinegar; the other one is filled with mustard and dill, then marinated in sugar and vinegar before dusting it with rye flour and frying it. We do that every year at Christmas and Easter, but we also do it for lunch here, because it's very similar to a typical Danish lunch.

Did you eat a lot of pickled herring when you were growing up?

We ate it every Saturday and Sunday for lunch at my parents' house. When you grow up with those kinds of things, it's part of your palate and your story.

What do you consider to be traditional Danish dishes?

Traditional Danish foods are made with ingredients found here. We have ocean surrounding us on all sides, so we eat a lot of herring and other fish. We also love pork here in Denmark. Of course, we use a lot of vegetables: cabbage, onions, anything that can be found in the wintertime. In the summertime, we have all kinds of fruits and vegetables, but that's only for a few months a year. In Denmark, we balance sweet and sour. We love that. Here we serve chicken with pickled cucumbers and marinated rhubarbs; it's sweet and sour.

Are the long winters why pickling is such a big part of Danish cuisine?

To be honest, now everything is pickled, fermented, smoked, and so on, the way it was a long, long time ago. Pickling is back in style.

What do you think about the New Nordic food movement?

I think it's on its way out. It's been in fashion for 10 years, and it's time to move on. If you've been eating the same flavors for 10 years, you know exactly what you're going to get at each restaurant. It's getting boring. The next step is going to be all about showing what we can actually do as chefs—how we cook instead of just how we decorate things.

Do you think many other people share that same view as you?

I was just in New York, and when you say

13

you're from Denmark, all of the sudden you're friends right away. New York wants to be Copenhagen and Copenhagen wants to be New York.

Do you think that there's going to be a tendency for restaurants to kind of look back and see what Danish food was before the New Nordic movement, and maybe restore some of those dishes?

I hope not. It would be like looking back on a dated outfit; you don't want to wear something that's out of fashion. You want to wear something special—and often that means being yourself and not conforming to a group ideal anymore. If you are identified as part of New Nordic cuisine, you run the risk of being stuck in that part. If you want to move forward, you have to build your own kitchen up again by being yourself. You cannot just eat flowers. New Nordic will have to evolve into more than just pretty decoration.

How important is it for a dish to look good?

Of course, you eat with your eyes first. In summertime, a plate has to be green. The plate should show what time period you're in. Right now, it's freezing here, so it's okay if I'm not putting fresh herbs on the plate—because there are none. Everyone does it his or her own way; I think it's important to show some personality in it.

Are your customers mostly Danish or foreign?

In the winter, it's mostly Danish people, but we get lots of visitors from China.

What's your favorite dish to cook at the restaurant?

Right now, it's the pork belly. It really is a perfect Danish dish because it has distinctly Danish flavors. We score the pork belly and it results in a crispy top layer. I love it with the side dish: this incredible marinated wet cabbage with brown potatoes and a good brown sauce. It's really a perfect combination.

If you could cook for any chef who's ever lived, who would it be and why?

Charlie Trotter. In the 1990s, he was even bigger than René [Redzepi of Noma] is now. He was doing some amazing things back then.

What do you cook at home when you're not at the restaurant?

Mexican food, actually. My wife is half-Mexican, and I really love Mexican food. It's totally different from what we do here, because of the heat, the flour, and the stories. Everything has to be done in a certain way. Two months ago, we actually had tacos on the menu. We were making them tableside.

Balsamic Marinated Herrings

Recipe by John Kofod Pedersen from Sortebro Kro.

In Denmark, we eat herrings almost every day. This recipe is almost 20 years old, and is prepared for Christmas at the restaurant. It's one of my favorites.

Prep time: 2 days
Cooking time: 5 minutes
Assembly: 5 minutes
Serves: 6

Combine all ingredients except for herring and apple in a medium saucepan, and bring to a boil over medium-high heat.

Reduce heat and simmer until sugar dissolves, about 5 minutes.

Remove from heat and allow the pickling liquid to cool to room temperature. Refrigerate.

Place herring fillets in a non-reactive bowl. Pour in cooled pickling liquid and stir to combine. Let marinate for 2 days.

To serve, remove fillets from the pickling liquid and pat dry. Cut fillets into 3-inch pieces and transfer to a platter.

Garnish with red onion, apples, and fresh dill.

10	salted herring fillets (approx. 1.2 kg), rinsed, soaked in water overnight, and drained
750 g	balsamic vinegar
600 g	brown sugar
2	bay leaves
2	red onions, thinly sliced
1	bunch fresh thyme
1	bunch fresh dill
20	whole black peppercorns
5 g	allspice
1	cinnamon stick
10	cloves
1	red apple, diced

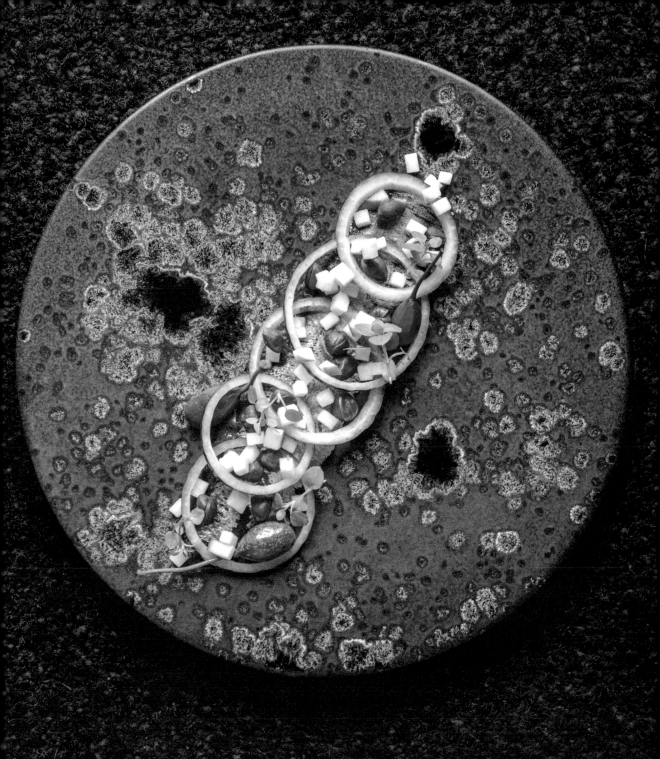

Mustard and Dill
Herring Fillets

Recipe by John Kofod Pedersen from Sortebro Kro.

This recipe has been with the restaurant since we first opened. It is typically served at lunch during holidays such as Easter and Christmas. It's not expensive, very easy to make, and hits the spot every time.

Prep time: 1 hour
Cooking time: 1 hour
Assembly: 5 minutes
Serves: 4

With skin side down, slather a thick layer of mustard on the interior of the fillets, and sprinkle with fresh, chopped dill.

Roll fillets in rye flour.

Add butter to skillet on high heat and fry fish on each side until golden brown. Salt to taste.

Set fried herring aside.

Combine pickle marinade ingredients in a pot. Stir over medium heat until sugar is completely dissolved.

Pour marinade over herring and onion. Cover with plastic wrap or a lid and let sit at room temperature until you have to serve it the same day. If you want to keep it in the fridge, make sure marinade is covered.

To serve, place fried herring on a plate and garnish with onion rings, capers, fresh herbs, grated horseradish, and apples.

500 g	fresh herring fillets, skin on, fins removed
200 ml	rye flour
150 g	butter
1	large bunch fresh dill
200 ml	mustard
1/2	red onion
1	red apple in small dices

PICKLE MARINADE

500 ml	white wine vinegar (24%)
500 ml	caster sugar
5 g	whole allspice
1	pinch of salt
1	bay leaf
10	whole black peppercorns
1	horseradish root
1	bunch thyme
1	bunch coriander
1	bunch basil
1	bunch dill

The Pølse of a Nation
By Jonathan Shipley

Even though you've just finished a full dinner, a late-night spin through Tivoli Gardens has you hungry again. You're eyeing every convenience store like a hawk as you stroll down Vesterbrogade, staving off the inexplicably strong growls coming from your gut. Until you reach a hot dog stand. No matter the time of day or where you are in the country—from Herning to Helsingør, Svendborg to Sønderborg—you know you can always find a hot dog. They've been hot in Denmark for nearly 100 years.

Here they're called pølse, and the hot dog stands that serve them—pølsevogens, or "sausage wagons"—are universally loved. "My favorite childhood memories involve going down to Horsens center and having a bright-red hot dog," says Martin Hoeedholt, a self-proclaimed pølse pioneer who founded his own Danish-style hot dog stand in New York City. Owner of Revolving Dansk, he was raised in Horsens, Denmark and studied at the Århus School of Business before moving to New York City in 2001. It didn't take long to realize, much to his chagrin, that he could not find his pølse in America. As he describes it, he now brings "meat to the streets" of Manhattan and Brooklyn.

Denmark's love for hot dogs started with Charles Svendsen Stevns. It was the early 1920s and the Danish mob had a chokehold on Copenhagen's restaurants, strong-arming restaurateurs with price-fixing and kickbacks. To compensate, restaurants had to charge more, and these climbing costs prevented the Danish working class from eating out.

Around the same time, landlords of the 1920s and 1930s were concerned that cooking was a fire hazard, so they refused restaurant owners as tenants for fear that their properties would, quite literally, go up in flames. And that's when Stevns began serving up cheap, hot meals to families hungry to get out of the house for a meal—to see and be seen.

Thanks to the early and long-time success of Stevns' cart and a dire need to lessen the mob's growing (and stifling) influence, Copenhagen city hall legalized pølsevogens. The plan worked, and the

mob's tight grip on dining loosened. Wagons proliferated until they were everywhere. Food was carried and eaten in hand—without formal table seating. The humble hot dog helped take down the mob bosses.

By the mid-20th century there were 600 hot dog carts in Denmark. And at peak pølse, Copenhagen had 800 sausage wagons on corners throughout the capital city alone. The carts were king, all offering affordable meals for working folks. A few kroner could buy lunch.

Danes loved their hot dogs, but they really loved the accessibility of cheap food. By the 1980s, hot dogs weren't the only option in Copenhagen that met that need. American fast food restaurants were putting down roots in Denmark and taking a sizeable bite out of hot dog profits.

At the same time, Copenhagen, was putting Scandinavia on the map as a major dining destination outside of France and Italy, as Danish chefs, who trained in those countries, returned home with new techniques at their disposal. Slowly, Danes became willing to pay more for finer dining, for the expertise of the chefs who served them, and the rare ingredients they presented.

Hot dog cart lights dimmed, relegated as backwater grub for the after-party crowd or those for whom fine dining was still out of reach. The rise of New Nordic cuisine in the early aughts didn't help: Pitting hot dogs against elaborate preparations of roasted wild duck and mahogany clams.

But classics are classic for a reason, and even the chefs at the city's haughtiest fine dining restaurants stop by hot dog stands for a taste of the distinctly Danish food they know and love. Claus Christensen, owner of a pølsevogen serving organic hot dogs near the iconic Rundetaarn in downtown Copenhagen, knows: "The chefs at restaurant Noma have ordered my hot dogs as midnight snacks. They know what good food is."

Approximately 100 million hot dogs are eaten each year in Denmark, even though only 5.5 million people live in the country. And everyone has their preferences. Christensen opts for the classic, a hot dog piled high with toppings, including ketchup, mustard, remoulade (mayonnaise combined with pickled vegetables), fresh and roasted onions, and gherkins. Then there's the fransk dog, a hollowed out baguette stuffed with a hot dog and smothered in mayonnaise, oftentimes tinged with horseradish or paprika. Some scarf down a medisterpølse, laced with allspice, cloves, salt and pepper for a spicier kick than the average dog, or a pølse i svob, a hot dog wrapped in bacon. Many wash them down with some cold Cocio brand chocolate milk: the go-to beverage for a hot dog meal. All Danes, no matter where they come from, meet at the carts and eat, united for those brief (delicious) moments in time—then go their separate ways.

At the tail end of the fine dining overhaul in Denmark, the beloved hot dog is due for a tune up. Maybe it'll come from one of the remaining 100 sausage wagons dotting Copenhagen's sidewalks. Or maybe it'll come from the high-end chefs who have radically transformed Denmark into a world-renowned culinary destination.

But it could just result from experimentation at the Danish Hot Dog Championships, an event held each year in Århus, Denmark dedicated to celebrating the country's favorite tubed meat. Ole Troelsø, food and restaurant editor at the Copenhagen-based business daily, Børsen, who has eaten at—and reviewed—more than 500 gourmet restaurants worldwide, started the event, and is giving the country's high-end chefs reason to elevate and celebrate the Danish dog. Paul Cunningham, chef of The Paul and Henne Kirkeby Kro, has won the festival's main event several times. So has Jeppe Foldager, chef at Alberto K atop Copenhagen's Radisson Blu Royal Hotel whose award sits next to the silver statuette he earned at the Bocuse d'Or. This is to say, pølse has earned its beloved position not just as a quick snack, but as a source of inspiration, even among the most influential, contemporary chefs, and has endeared itself as a traditional food deeply embedded in Danish culture.

These days, Denmark's favorite street food is also becoming one of the country's most prized exports. There are dozens of Danish sausage wagons in Russia, and their influence stretches from Germany to Singapore. Wherever they're consumed, they're stuffed with reminders of home, somewhere on the cobblestone streets of the Danish capital, where customers young and old line up for pølse made the way they crave it. "My favorite hot dog memories?" Christensten thinks, "The one that makes an elderly customer say that eating my hot dog makes him want to eat hot dogs again."

Nicolai Nørregaard

KADEAU, COPENHAGEN
55.67229° N, 12.58897° E

Born Home:
Nicolai Nørregaard of Kadeau

"Bornholm is a fucking amazing island," says Nicolai Nørregaard, chef-owner of Kadeau. He was born on this Danish island in the Baltic Sea southeast of Sweden. "Ask any Dane. Everything is different there." It's a holiday island, where the summers are longer, filled with mulberries and figs, and where a warmer climate stretches into fall—a rarity in Scandinavia, where winters are usually long, cold, and dark. Part of the island is rocky and wild; another part is home to pristine sand beaches; and the rest is covered with forest and field. Knowing that they grew up with better nature and better products on Bornholm than they'd experienced anywhere else, Nørregaard and his lifelong friend Rasmus Kofoed vowed that if they ever got the chance to open a restaurant together, they had to do it on Bornholm. In 2007, the promise was realized, and their new restaurant, christened Kadeau, welcomed its first guests.

They hadn't fully committed to what we now know as a New Nordic obsession with hyperlocal sourcing when the original Kadeau opened. The early dishes made use of local dairy, meat, and vegetables, but it wasn't until they hit their stride three years later that they incorporated flora and far-out foraging. "That's when we got crazy with it," Nørregaard jokes.

"Nobody was really doing it yet," remembers Nørregaard of those early times, narrowing their scope to using only Bornholm products, instead of products that came from Scandinavia at large. "We basically pickled, fermented, and preserved all of Bornholm. What we couldn't get from Bornholm, we got from the rest of Denmark. But Bornholm really became the backbone of our cooking."

Until Kadeau relocated to Copenhagen in 2011.

When Nørregaard and Kofoed started having kids, they realized it would be better to raise them in Copenhagen and move the restaurant. Still, the dedication to Bornholm cooking moved with them. "Everything started on Bornholm, and it's still Bornholm that's the core of our cooking," says Nørregaard. "This year we pickled six tons of Bornholm products and made everything from syrups to vinegars, using mushrooms, vegetables, wildflowers, and honeys from the island."

The only thing that stayed put on the island was a focus on meat. The new Kadeau (which has since graduated to a larger space next door to its first location in Copenhagen) touted a vegetable-based menu. There's good reason for that: On Bornholm, they had a slaughterhouse where they butchered local lambs, wild pigs, and cows. When it closed down, they couldn't butcher on Bornholm anymore. "The only solution was to put the animals on the ferry, sail them to Sweden, drive them through Sweden to Denmark, only to send the meat to a freezer. It was just horrible," Nørregaard says in disgust.

The tension that arises from the need to be flexible while staying true to his convictions, as well as the inspiration he draws from his life in the city and his upbringing on the island, are what makes Nørregaard's cooking unique. He attributes the ease with which he flits between those opposites to his lack of formal culinary training. It keeps him creative. "The lack of formal training, and my upbringing, make it easier for me to think outside of the box. I have no restrictions."

Black Currant Leaves, Wood Sorrel, and Kohlrabi

Recipe by Nicolai Nørregaard from Kadeau.

A couple of years ago, we planted a small garden for the restaurant. Now we have a huge garden with hundreds of berry bushes that is managed by my father, his wife, and the bees, of course. One our favorite things is the black currant bush. It is actually not the berry itself that is the most interesting thing for us. It is the leaves. They taste more of black currant than the berry ever will. The luxury of having a garden is getting fantastic products, like those black currant leaves, that you couldn't buy for all the money in the world.

Prep time: 14 days
Cooking time: 2 hours
Assembly: 10 minutes
Serves: 4

Pickled black currant leaves:

Bring water, vinegar, and sugar to a boil. When the sugar is dissolved, refrigerate.

Once cooled, pour the cold pickling liquid over the leaves in a glass jar.

Put a round plastic lid or something inside the jar to sink the leaves under the surface. Keep refrigerated. Wait for at least 2 days before using.

Black currant leaf oil:

Blend the oil and the leaves on high speed for 2 minutes.

Wait 30 minutes until straining through a fine-mesh sieve.

Store oil in small bags in freezer to keep fresh.

Fermented peas:

Blend peas with water on high speed for 30 seconds.

Wait 30 minutes and strain through a fine-mesh sieve.

Dissolve the salt in the liquid with an immersion blender. Put the liquid in a jar with a mesh or cloth and a lid.

Leave the jar at room temperature for 3 days.

Strain and refrigerate.

•••

PICKLED BLACK CURRANT LEAVES

1	jar black currant leaves
500 g	spirit vinegar (6% acidity)
250 g	water
175 g	caster sugar

BLACK CURRANT LEAF OIL

100 g	black currant leaves
200 g	grapeseed oil

FERMENTED PEAS

300 g	green peas without pods
200 g	water
6 g	salt

PICKLED FIGS

1	jar figs, half ripe
500 g	spirit vinegar (6% acidity)
250 g	water
175 g	caster sugar

PICKLED FIREWEED FLOWER BUDS

1	jar fireweed flowers, unbloomed and still on the branch
500 g	spirit vinegar (6% acidity)
250 g	water
175 g	caster sugar

Black Currant Leaves, Wood Sorrel, and Kohlrabi - *continuation*

Pickled figs:

Bring water, vinegar, and sugar to a boil. When the sugar is dissolved, refrigerate.

Make 10 small holes in the skin of the figs with a needle.

Pour cold pickling liquid over the figs in a glass jar. Put round plastic lid or weight inside the jar to press down the figs under the surface.

Keep refrigerated. Wait two weeks before using.

Before serving, halve the figs. Cut thinly into 3 mm slices with a half moon shape.

Pickled fireweed flower buds:

Bring water, vinegar, and sugar to a boil. When the sugar is dissolved, refrigerate.

Pour the cold pickling liquid over the fireweed in a glass jar.

Put a round plastic lid or a weight inside the jar to press down the flowers under the surface. Keep refrigerated.

Wait two days before using. Before serving, pick the buds from the branch.

Wood sorrel purée:

Make just before serving.

Blend wood sorrel and spinach for 4 minutes.

Add water until desired texture is achieved. Make sure to scrape the edges once in a while.

Salt to taste.

...

WOOD SORREL PUREE

100 g	wood sorrel leaves
75 g	blanched spinach
1	spinch of salt

RAZOR CLAM SAUCE

5	razor clams
60 g	gooseberry wine
50 g	gooseberry juice
50 g	fermented peas, juice
1/2	leaf gelatin
5 g	black currant leaf pickle juice
1	pinch of salt

SALTED CABBAGE

2	white cabbage leaves
1	pinch of salt

KOHLRABI

1	small kohlrabi

Black Currant Leaves, Wood Sorrel, and Kohlrabi – *continuation*

Razor clam sauce:

Steam the clams in 50 g of gooseberry wine until they open in a casserole. Add just enough water to cover. Simmer for 30 minutes.

Pull it off the heat. Wait one hour and strain through a fine-mesh sieve.

Reduce until 50 g remains.

Soak gelatin in cold water. Dissolve it in the 50 g of boiling stock.

Add fermented pea juice, black currant pickle juice, gooseberry juice, and gooseberry wine. Taste with salt. Refrigerate. When it is set, strain it through a fine-mesh sieve to make it liquid again.

Salted cabbage:

Bring 5 liters of 3 percent salted water to a boil.

Cook the cabbage for 2 minutes and put it in ice water.

Drain it and cut in a half moon shape with different sizes, between approximately 3 and 4.5 cm long. Refrigerate.

Kohlrabi:

Slice kohlrabi thinly, approximately 3 mm each.

Cut in half moon shapes with different sizes, between approximately 3 and 3.4 cm long.

Put in container with water. Refrigerate.

Plating:

Make a circle of wood sorrel purée in the middle of the plate.

Arrange cabbage, kohlrabi, and figs inside the circle, pointing in the same direction.

Arrange black currant leaves on top with wrinkly side facing up. Add fireweed buds.

Add a spoonful of black currant leaf oil to the sauce.

Only top dish with sauce while serving, approximately 1.5 tbsp. per plate.

Kale, Hemp, and Grilled Oysters

Recipe by Nicolai Nørregaard from Kadeau.

The type of hemp we use is packed with flavor and does not contain any THC. Few people know about the culinary applications of hemp: Its aroma and flavor pair brilliantly with mollusks from the waters that surround Denmark. At Kadeau, we serve hemp with Limfjorden oysters alongside kale from the garden that we blanch in water to taste more like the ocean. My father handpicks the finishing touch: hazelnuts, which give crunch and texture to the dish.

Prep time: 2 days
Cooking time:
Assembly: 2 mins
Serves: 4

Parsley oil:

Heat oil and parsley to 80°C on medium heat. When it reaches that temperature, blend for 10 minutes and strain.

Hemp:

Blend oil and leaves on high speed for 2 minutes. Pack oil with pulp in an airtight bag. Store the oil in the fridge for at least 2 days and strain just before use.

Pea powder:

Dry the peas at 45°C for 24 hours, or until dry. Blend into a fine powder. Keep away from light (the freezer works well) to maintain color.

Oyster vinaigrette:

Shuck oysters and preserve their water in a separate container.

Chop oysters into 3 mm pieces. Add hazelnuts, parsley, lemon juice, along with a spoonful of hemp and parsley oil. Add salt to taste.

The mixture keeps for 24 hours in the fridge.

Oyster emulsion:

Shuck the oysters and preserve the water in a separate container.

Blend oysters with lemon juice and half of the oyster water. While blending, slowly drizzle oil into the mixture. Add salt to taste.

Adjust texture with oyster brine; finished sauce should be thick and creamy.

This emulsion keeps for 24 hours in the fridge.

•••

PARSLEY OIL

50 g	parsley leaves, rinsed and drained
100 g	grapeseed oil

HEMP OIL

50 g	hemp leaves, rinsed and drained
100 g	grapeseed oil

PEA POWDER

250 g	green peas, fresh

OYSTER VINAIGRETTE

2	oysters including the brine
25 g	chopped parsley
25 g	chopped fresh hazelnuts
1/2	lemon, juice
1	pinch of salt

OYSTER EMULSION

4	oysters, including the brine
1/2	lemon (for juice)
100-150 g	grapeseed oil
1	pinch of salt

Grilled oysters:

Start a fire with beechwood. Grill oysters over flames. Depending on the size and type of oyster, grill with lid on for 1 to 3 minutes, then flip, grilling for 1 to 3 minutes more.

They will be done when steam begins escaping from the shell. Manually open the oyster if hasn't opened yet.

Discard the fleshy gray part of the oyster and cut the large, white muscle into 4 even slices approximately 2 minutes before plating.

Blanched kale bunches:

Just before serving, assemble kale bunches, with the largest leaf at the bottom and the smallest leaf at the top. Make four bunches.

Bring the water to a boil. Remove from heat and add kombu, dulse, and salt to water. Let rest for 30 minutes.

Heat the water to 90°C. Fold each kale bunch in a shape similar to a taco. Using tweezers, working bunch by bunch, blanch for 20 seconds.

Plating:

Put a spoonful of oyster emulsion in the center of the plate.

Unfold the warm, blanched kale bunch to sit on top of emulsion, and add 4 slices of grilled oyster, as well as one spoonful of oyster vinaigrette.

Fold it again.

Dust with pea powder and put the cabbage bunch onto the emulsion, covering halfway to serve.

GRILLED OYSTERS

4 *oysters*

BLANCHED KALE BUNCHES

6 *leaves from different types of kale and mustard, rinsed*

3000 g *water*

30 g *kombu, dried*

30 g *dulse, dried*

60 g *salt*

René Redzepi

NOMA, COPENHAGEN
55.67789° N, 12.59629° E

René Redzepi's reputation precedes him. As it should: He's the crown prince of New Nordic cooking and the face of Restaurant Noma, where he is chef and co-founder. If Noma is the most influential restaurant in the world right now, Redzepi may well be the world's most influential chef. You can't talk about eating in Denmark without him.

At Noma, Redzepi commands a bustling kitchen bursting with talent that's pushing the boundaries of Nordic cuisine using as many local ingredients as possible. He oversees an internal research and development lab, where obscure insects from the backyard are fermented and new hybrid plants are born. But it all starts with the menu, which is created in the room where we're sitting. It's what he describes as an innovation lab that also functions as a multi-purpose space for his staff. This is where they eat together and hang-out together. It's used as a changing room as well as an office. "It's maybe not much of a lab, but it is dedicated to new thinking," he says. Really, it's where the magic happens.

Noma is often considered to be one of the most influential restaurants in the world. Why do you think that is?

I don't agree with that. Technically, McDonald's is a restaurant as well, and it's much more influential—it really feeds a lot of people. But, within a small group of foodies, we do have a special voice—and people are listening. It also helps, especially nowadays, that we are good at communicating all of this. We have things to say, and we know how to say it.

Why is doing this especially important today?

We happened to come into the world at a specific time, when the food world was looking for something fresh to write about. The world was also really opening, and there was a shift away from a very traditional focus on France and Italy. It was the explosion of the [World's 50 Best Restaurant list].

Suddenly, the foodies of the world were interested in what restaurants in Scandinavia had to say. Not only Scandinavia, but also, suddenly, places in Mexico were revered with as much respect as the ones in New York. Restaurants in Chile and São Paolo were also part of the world map. It was a real explosion—as if the world opened all at once, and we happened to be there at that specific moment, trying to define something from our region.

Around what year was that?

There was also a terrible financial crisis at that time, around 2007 or 2008. After that, there was this natural urge to gravitate toward places that were safe havens, societies in which they've figured it out somehow: Places that were close to nature, where there's a nice democratic system, where the social aspects of living were special. I actually think that gave

Scandinavia extra attention during that period. People wanted all things Scandinavian, and couldn't get enough, whether it was just the idea of Nordic food or design, philosophy, proximity to nature, handcrafted wood. And it's not going away anytime soon; Denmark is on the map.

What kind of influence has the San Pellegrino's World's 50 Best Restaurants list had on Noma?

Nobody would give a shit about us if it weren't for that list. I don't believe we're the best; I don't believe we've ever been the best. I don't believe there is even such a thing as the best restaurant in the world. Lists are silly. Judging flavor and taste is very difficult; most of the time, it's also very pretentious and stupid when you really think about it. But, when I envision the world without the Pellegrino list, I see a very boring place. I see a place exactly like it was 15 years ago, before the list opened the world the way that it did.

For Scandinavia, it changed the economy of a region. Will it do that again for another region? I don't think so, but it can maybe happen for whoever makes it to the top five.

You're active on social media. What role has the internet played in the growth of the restaurant?

We're the first generation of restaurants to be in the crossfire of traditional media and new media—figuring out where we fit in, how we can communicate both ways. Before, we used to craft these press messages, and you'd be lucky if a bit of what you wanted to say made it in there. Today, you're in control of everything. You have your own accounts. When I used to travel, I would buy guidebooks. I never do that anymore. I follow people who actually live in the places and go out a lot on social media.

It is a brave new world that is just going to keep growing. If you're a restaurant, and you're not part of that, you're doing something very wrong. Think about it: We were sort of adults when this all exploded. Now imagine people who grew up with this; if you don't have it, you're going to be invisible.

How would you describe your style of cooking?

I wish I had a straight answer to that, but I don't. We're still very much taking our baby steps and figuring it out, even after 12 successful years. Ultimately, what we're trying to do is work with a flavor or region and bring forth creativity and new thinking.

What has made you proudest during the 12 years you've been at Noma?

One is an appreciation for wild landscape. We've discovered a new range of ingredients by being connected to it, exploring it, and codifying it. We've connected a generation of chefs to place and seasonality. And I know all the jokes about putting weeds on my plate and all of that. But when you do something new, there will always be moments where you're unsure if what you're doing is right. That feeling doesn't go away.

The second thing is that we have taken old preservation methods and amplified them, making them the new building blocks for our cuisine. It's food engineering through preservation and fermentation. That idea is really exploding right now. We're just now scratching the surface of all this weird stuff. We don't even understand what it all does to your internal system—your brain, your gut. I would really like to explore all that.

One last thing: We brought chef-waiter connectivity to the restaurant experience. Twelve years ago, the idea of chefs serving diners was considered a very weird thing.

How local is local?

We're not that local. Sometimes, we get things from Iceland. I don't know what it means. I haven't figured it out. In the

search for the answer, you also discover that a lot of the labels that define cooking are so vague and ill-defined. What is it to be local? What is molecular gastronomy? What's farm-to-table? And what's the best model? And how do you cook best? And how do you cook something unique? And how do you tap into and support a local community?

What was it like taking Noma on the road, to Tokyo and then to Sydney?

We just free-fall into a new place. But after Tokyo, I was more confident. I finally understood that this business is a marathon, and we have put on our training shoes and stop worrying. We don't have to be so doubtful all the time because innovation in food culture is a slow, grinding process; only through that process does it become meaningful. You really see that in Japan: the slow grind of innovation keeps the food relevant. They're challenging it ever so slightly all the time, and never let their traditions turn stale. I was blown away by that.

Even the smallest menial tasks yield huge potential there. An example of that in Japan is Zen Buddhism. They codified the tea ceremony because drinking a cup of tea, repeating everyday actions, could bring you closer to spiritual enlightenment and give your life meaning. It could make you enjoy things you already do every day. That birthed a whole tradition: a new style of room and architecture, a new style of bowing because the top of the doorframe was low, and a whole new cuisine. The unpleasant feeling of drinking intense tea on an empty stomach birthed kaiseki, which some people say is the birth of the tasting menu in the West. Imagine: all that from a cup of tea.

Has the format of the menu at Noma changed since you returned from Japan?

We shortened the menu: Larger servings, not so many small things. It's something we've been thinking about for years, but Japan made us confident enough to do it. It's also probably an age thing too. When you're younger, you think it's about showing off: "Here's my large menu, and I'll give you so much food. I can keep going if you want to," as opposed to trying to focus on the real essential stuff you actually want to serve.

What happens in the research and development lab at Noma?

Putting it simply, we're just fooling around. If you want to be more philosophical about it, it is a place where we try to make sense of the failures that inevitably happen in a creative endeavor. On a day-to-day level, we get ingredients and process them. We try to just use our past knowledge and current creativity to figure out how to express a piece of food in a new and fantastic way that relates to our place, our history, and the season. We want guests to feel all of those things at the same time. It's very difficult— we hardly ever reach that level. But, sometimes, we do—and those moments are special.

You've mentioned in the past that food has to take care of you—that it's important how a diner feels a day or two after a meal. What do you mean by that?

It's a very different focus than I was taught as a cook. There used to be this implied feeling that going out for that great meal—a true fine dining meal—meant you had to fuck yourself up. But somehow it was okay because it was all a quest for flavor. So what if you sat on the toilet next day with a horrible stomachache? I think we fucked up there. And, I'm not saying that people aren't full when they leave Noma, but at one point, diners do think, "I'm not feeling good." So we're trying to give people food that's not just flavorful, but also nutritious.

How do you cook at home?

I cook very simply at home, and use a lot of fermentation as well. My at-home meals are vegetable-based, and they're always cooked meals. The way I like to eat is 98% vegetable and 2% fish. My whole life is food. Nowadays, people are very busy and don't have time to cook—or at least feel like they don't have time to cook. I'm the opposite. We have three-course meals for our hour and 15-minute staff break. It's important to sit down, eat, and give yourself some fuel that makes you want to stand up and do something.

If you could cook for any chef, dead or alive, who would it be?

Paul Bocuse. I think he's the coolest. He has been able to stay on top for 50 years and is somehow still able to connect with young people. His staff shows the same rigor every day they go to work. They do what they do exceptionally well, and they're proud of it. They're not burned out, and you can taste that. I would love to have him come to the restaurant, show him to his table, take out his chair, have him sit down, and ask him what he wants today. He's a megastar in my book. He's like our culinary granddad.

Poached Danish Oysters, Steamed Summer Cabbage, and Black Currant

Recipe by René Redzepi from Noma.

Prep time: 6 weeks
Cooking time: 2 hours
Assembly: 15 mins
Serves: 4

Poached Danish oysters:

Bring a pot of salted water to boil.

Blanch oysters in the shell for 90 seconds then shock immediately in ice water to ensure that they cool down completely before opening.

Carefully shuck oysters, separating the flesh from the guts and removing any remaining pieces of shell.

Place oysters in a container over ice and refrigerate.

Salted unripe black currants:

Place unripe black currants and salt in a vacuum bag, gently agitating contents to ensure for an even distribution of salt. Seal the vacuum bag on maximum and store in the fridge for a minimum of 6 weeks.

Black currant leaf oil:

Roughly chop black currant leaves into smaller pieces and transfer to a blender with the grapeseed oil poured over top.

Blend for 7 minutes on high speed. When the oil has finished blending, the temperature will have risen to almost 70°C. Chill as as quickly as possible.

Transfer oil to a stainless steel bowl. Place bowl over ice water and stir until mixture is cold.

Allow oil to sit refrigerated overnight in a plastic container and strain through a cheesecloth the following day .

...

4	*large oysters (approx. 250 g each)*
200 g	*unripe black currants (other unripe berries or buds can be substituted in place of black currants)*
16 g	*finely ground non iodized salt (8% by weight)*
225 g	*dark green black currant leaves (or flat leaf parsley)*
330 g	*grapeseed oil*
10	*lovage leaves*
2	*small heads of pointed summer cabbages (choose younger cabbages approximately 15-20 cm in length with paler yellow leaves at their hearts, as they will be sweeter and juicier once cooked)*

Steamed tender summer cabbage:

Remove outer leaves of summer cabbage and clean heads of any remaining dirt.

Place cabbage, 30g of salted unripe black currants, 40g of salted unripe currant juice, and 40g of black currant leaf oil in a vacuum bag and seal on maximum.

Let cabbage cure in the bags for 2 hours. Then steam in bag for about 2 minutes.

Once cooked, remove, and shock immediately in ice water.

To plate:

Slice cooked oysters lengthwise into 1 cm strips.

Pull cabbage from bags and remove any capers and excess juices.

Collect any small pieces of cabbage and cabbage juice from the bag and reserve.

Slice the base off of the cabbage so that the leaves of the heart may fall freely from the core.

Arrange leaves of cabbage, rib side down, around the plate.

Drape the slices of 1 oyster at different angles in the cabbage leaf cups and directly onto the plate as well.

Drizzle the oil, juices, and unripe black currant capers over top of the plate.

Garnish with finely chopped lovage.

Glazed Celeriac with Brown Butter and Buttermilk Sauce

Recipe by Nadine Redzepi from Noma.

René Redzepi cooks for the world. But who cooks for René Redzepi? In his Copenhagen apartment, it's mostly Nadine Levy Redzepi, his wife. She's the former booking manager at Noma (yes, she's the one who likely denied your reservation) and an upcoming cookbook author, who relies less on tweezers and fermented weeds from the backyard and focuses instead on pairing everyday ingredients in unexpected ways. Take, for example, this vegetable-forward recipe, in which beef accompanies celeriac (not the other way around), and is tied together by a silky, tangy buttermilk-brown butter sauce.

Prep time: 30 mins
Cooking time: 1 hour, 20 minutes
Assembly: 5 minutes
Serves: 2

Set oven to 170°C.

Peel celeriac and cut into 4 even pieces (into quarters, not into round disks).

Drizzle oil into a pan that can later go into the oven (i.e., one without a plastic handle).

Place the celeriac with flat surface down and put in the oven for about 20 min before turning celeriac onto the other flat side.

While the celeriac is in the oven start browning the butter; put a medium size pan (do not use a Teflon pan) over medium heat, cut the butter into small pieces and put in the pan.

While the celeriac is in the oven, put a medium-sized pan on the burner over medium heat. Cut butter into small pieces and drop into the pan. Using a flat whisk, stir butter around. Shortly after all butter has melted, it will begin to form bubbles and foam on the top. At this point, whisking should be constant. When butter begins to smell nutty, lift the pan off the heat and gently tip the pan to one side. If there are brown sediments in the pan, you have succeeded.

Quickly pour the brown butter into a bowl to prevent it from cooking further and set aside.

Turn the celeriac to sit on the other flat side.

Toast the pine nuts in a pan over medium-high heat and set aside.

In a small pot, heat oil over medium-high heat. Tear the leaves off the stem of the kale and cut them into small pieces, about the size of a coin.

•••

1	whole peeled celeriac
150 ml	beef glaze / stock
2	large kale leaves
200 g	pine nuts, toasted
115 g	butter
100-150 ml	buttermilk
50 g	parmesan, for grating
200 ml	neutral frying oil (such as canola, grapeseed, or peanut oil)

Take the pan out of the oven, turn the celeriac onto the other side again and pour half of the beef glaze into the pan. Baste celeriac with glaze a few times and put back in the oven. Turn oven up to 200°C.

Put small pieces of kale into hot oil on the stove. While the kale is in the oil (it will likely splatter), lay paper towels out on counter.

Remove the kale once the color changes from a deep green to a more translucent, seaweed-like green. Place kale on paper towels to drain excess oil.

Turn the celeriac over again and add the rest of the glaze, and baste it again.

Continue doing this every 5-10 minutes until you can stick a sharp knife through the pieces. Once you can stick a knife through the celeriac, take the pan out of the oven and grate a generous amount of Parmesan over top.

Put back in the oven for 5 to 10 minutes.

While celeriac is finishing in the oven, gradually whisk buttermilk into brown butter.

In a bowl, pour in brown butter and buttermilk sauce. Add celeriac, and top with a generous amount of kale and pine nuts.

Season with salt and pepper to taste.

Christian Puglisi

RELÆ, COPENHAGEN
55.69302° N, 12.54329° E

We can barely keep up with Christian Puglisi. In the last five years alone, the Sicilian-Norwegian chef raised in Denmark has opened three blockbuster Copenhagen restaurants—Relæ, Manfreds & Vin, and Bæst—and published a cookbook. Sometimes he's firing up bubble-crusted, wood-oven pizzas and at other times he's managing a team that's turning out the city's most revered vegetable dishes. As if his body composition is pure adrenaline (and maybe wine), Puglisi does it all with a cool confidence, bucking expectations (for example, he's a vegetable-worshipper serving one of the world's best-known tartares) and not taking the expectations of New Nordic too seriously.

What was the original idea behind Relæ?

When we started, I wanted to do simple food, with two to three components maximum. Nobody wants to eat a dish where they lose track of what is going on. I wanted to make a high-end restaurant where we put a lot of effort into the food, but I wanted it to be more democratic with a lower price point, so it could be more approachable to a wider range of people.

How has that worked out so far?

To keep prices low, you have to question everything. Wages are much higher in Denmark than they are in New York. As a result, we have less freedom in the menu. Americans think it's a bit weird that there's no bar where they can wait and sip an aperitivo. I can only have about six bottles in the fridge at any given time. If I had a full bar, I would need a bartender, and that'd be expensive.

Vegetables are a part of that strategy too. A vegetable-focused menu is an easy way to have high quality food at a low price. Remember when everything was meat? And you would just have this loin rolled up and nicely poached as an entrée? Now, if we do lamb, we won't use that nice loin. We will use a less expensive cut, reduce the meat portion, and then cover it with vegetables. That's how that plating style came about—where everything is covered up. Because, underneath, we can find a way of combining the flavors in proportion in a way that's not about looks.

Obviously, when you really start getting a lot of experience doing this, you realize that lamb loin costs a lot, but the small herbs that we blend into a purée actually cost more. People still don't really understand that.

How would you describe your cooking?

Quality always needs to be at the fore of what we're doing, whether it's Nordic, Italian, whatever. Other things can be questioned—but never quality.

How do the open kitchens at your restaurants factor into the experience?

Originally, I just wanted to be in control of everything. I wanted to be able to see who came in, especially because I initially thought I'd be extremely lucky to have 20 people come in a day. At Bæst, we wanted people to be really close with the fire, the oven, and each other.

What was it like to work with Ferran Adria?

My time at el Bulli really changed me: my approach to cooking, food in general, restaurants. Everything was just turned upside down. The way they were questioning things was, for me, unheard of. Without having been there, I would probably think about food in a much more conventional way.

I remember my first day at El Bulli. Everyone had just arrived. It was 2006. When Ferran got there, it was like Jesus descending from the mount. It was very exciting; that year was epic.

How has your Italian background influenced your cooking?

My Italian background and the fact that I'm an immigrant influenced many things. It was one of the reasons I got off the Noma bus in 2009. To me, it didn't make sense at all do go down the New Nordic road. As an immigrant, I believed that a mix of styles and ingredients was important. Really: Does a potato need to be cultivated here for 10, 50, 300, or 500 years for it to be Nordic? There's a lot to be questioned in that arena if you're an immigrant. What I brought with me, cooking-wise, from Noma and Nordic cooking was the idea of running a light kitchen with vegetables.

What about hyperlocal sourcing?

Choosing rapeseed oil over olive oil doesn't really make sense to me. I think that's where it needs to be questioned. If I find an olive oil producer in Sicily who does everything right—makes great olive oil, does it organically—why wouldn't I opt for that? When I hear Australians saying, "Yeah, everything we use is from our continent," all I can think is: Good for you, it's fucking enormous.

How do you choose your products?

Quality is the only dogma.

What is Danish cuisine today?

It's hard for me to say, so I hope someone very intelligent will study it closely and tell me what the fuck is going on. Ten years ago, nothing was going on here. When I was a chef's apprentice I couldn't wait to get out of here. I wanted to go to a country where they actually made good food and had good produce. I remember wanting to go to Paris because they have chickens with legs and heads on.

Noma changed that. Rather than creating a restaurant scene based on the culture, we created something in a vacuum. You could actually create something new here. I don't think you could do that in Italy, where people are so conservative about what the right thing to do is.

So, you were never tempted to serve a grand, 30-course tasting menu?

In the beginning, we only did four-courses—some courses specifically for vegetarians and others with less restrictive diets. But, on day one, we had industry people and friends asking, "Can we just get everything?" Then the menu was suddenly seven courses, because people asked for it. Diners who didn't know us would've felt strange asking, so we instituted one four-course menu another seven-course menu. We have plans

of trying to do something a bit more extensive at the kitchen counter, but I fundamentally don't believe in very long menus.

Why don't you believe in them?

It takes more guts to trim and reduce. When you doubt yourself, you tend to add something: you guard yourself, sprinkle more on top. If you want to give people an experience that they can remember clearly, there's a limit to how much you can throw at them. The optimal big experience menu should be somewhere between seven and 10 servings, no more than that.

Is there an ideal time limit to a meal?

We book people here for two-and-a-half hours. It's important to me to have a mix of young people who are just here eating our four-course menu with a glass of wine and older bigwigs coming from New York who want to try the whole shebang, asking us for more than what is offered on the menu. That diversity is important for the restaurant. And being able to get a gastronomic experience in two-and-a-half hours means diners can go out later or do something before; it's a substantive experience but it doesn't take up the whole night.

What do you cook at home?

I like to cook easy and fast. And I like to cook mostly vegetables. What I cook at home is probably closer to the food we serve at Manfreds than anything else. I like being able to just take a cabbage, cut it, steam it, and then top it with Parmesan and olive oil to serve alongside bread. I also try to reduce the amount of meat I eat from an ethical point of view. I also realize that I came from a place where we didn't eat much meat at home. In Sicily, all the meat you get is extremely thin slices, hammered even thinner, and then breaded. Steak is only for very special occasions.

Did you grow up around food?

My father worked in pizza places here when I was a kid so that will always be

special for me. I wanted to open a pizza place before I wanted to be a chef. But when we opened Relæ, I wanted to make sure it wasn't an Italian restaurant. There will never be pasta on the menu there. We didn't want to be in the New Nordic box either. We just want to create our own thing.

Oyster, Leek, and Leek Emulsion

Recipe by Christian Puglisi from Relæ.

Prep time: 2 hours
Cooking time: 1 hour
Assembly: 10 minutes
Serves: 6

Soft leeks:

Place a large pot of heavily salted water on high heat until it reaches a rolling boil.

Blanch leeks until the cores of the leeks are really soft, but not mushy, approximately 12 to 16 minutes, depending on the size of the leeks.

Transfer the leeks to salted ice water to cool.

Drain, then make an incision, lengthwise, into each leek so that you can separate the inner core and the outer layers of the leeks. Reserve the inner cores and cut them into 2 cm lengths.

Take the outer layers of the leeks and place them flat into a steamer in about five-sheet stacks.

Steam the leeks until they are soft enough to break when you pinch them between your fingers, approximately 12 to 16 minutes.

Let the leek sheets cool to room temperature.

...

18	large leeks, roots trimmed off, as well as green leaves removed and reserved for Leek Emulsion
500 g	neutral vegetable oil (such as canola, grapeseed, or peanut oil)
1	soft poached egg (cooked at 65°C for 25 mins)
50 g	egg yolks
20 g	lemon juice
5 g	salt
6	oysters, shucked, cleaned, and sliced into 0.5 cm lengths with oyster juice strained and reserved

Leek emulsion:

Preheat oven to 280°C.

Place green leaves in a single layer on baking trays and bake until they become completely charred and crispy, approximately 20 to 30 minutes.

Remove from oven and allow to cool.

Once cooled, crush dried leaves into a rough powder.

To make the oil infusion, place 100 g crushed dried green leaves into a thermal blender with 500 g neutral vegetable oil.

Set blender to 80°C and blend on high speed until it reaches 80°C .

Once it reaches 80°C, blend for 10 more minutes. Strain the oil through a fine-mesh strainer and allow to cool.

Pour poached egg and egg yolk into a blender and slowly pour in the cooled oil to emulsify.

Season with lemon juice and salt.

Finishing:

Dress reserved soft inner pieces of leek with the leek emulsion until well-coated and creamy. Season with lemon juice and salt.

Place leek pieces in the center of the plate. Place slices of oyster on top and season with salt and with a few firm sprays of lemon juice. Add more of the leek emulsion on top of the oyster.

Take the soft leeks' outer layers and fold them to resemble an oyster shell. Serve on top of the oyster shell, making several layers.

Season the oyster juice with lemon juice and brush on top of the leek. Season with salt and a few sprays of lemon juice.

Hokkaido Pumpkin, Sea Buckthorn, and Fresh Hazelnuts

Recipe by Christian Puglisi from Relæ.

Prep time: 1 day + 3 hours
Cooking time: 30 minutes
Assembly: 5 minutes
Serves: 6

Hokkaido pumpkin tartlets:

Trim the top and bottom of the Hokkaido pumpkin.

Cut the pumpkin in half, horizontally. Scoop out and discard the seeds.

Slice the pumpkin on the halved side, preferably using a meat slicer, to 0.75 mm slices.

Place pumpkin in large bowl on a scale and add salt to 1% of the weight of the pumpkin. Gently mix so that you do not break the slices. Allow slices to sit in the bowl until they soften slightly, approximately 15 to 20 minutes.

When they have softened, transfer slices into a vacuum bag and seal. Leave overnight in the fridge.

The next day, remove slices from the bag. They should be soft and pliable.

Starting with a wider slice, tear it so that you have a strip. Roll it into a cone-like shape tartlet with the skin side up. Take another slice, tear it so that you have another strip, and wrap that strip around the cone. Continue wrapping strips around until you have reached a 7 cm round.

Place the pumpkin tartlet into a parchment-lined 7 cm flan mold. Repeat this until you have six tartlets.

Preheat oven to 180°C.

Melt brown butter and spoon onto the tartlets.

Bake the tartlets for 15 to 20 minutes, until they are soft in the bottom center. Once cooked, remove them from the molds and, using a torch, char some of the top of the tartlets.

Spray with pear vinegar and season with a dash of salt.

•••

1	medium-large Hokkaido pumpkin or red kuri squash, at least 1.2 kg in weight
45 g	salt
60 g	brown butter
15 ml	pear vinegar
300 g	egg yolks
36	sea buckthorn berries
100 g	sea buckthorn juice
60 g	fresh hazelnuts, removed from shells

Egg yolk and sea buckthorn sauce:

Mix egg yolks and salt in a bowl. Transfer to a vacuum bag and seal. Cook in a water bath at 68°C for one hour, then cool down in an ice bath.

Once cooled, press cooked yolks through a fine-mesh sieve. Mix the cooked egg yolks with the sea buckthorn juice. Add salt to taste.

Fill a siphon bottle halfway and charge once. Place siphon in a water bath at 40°C until warm, at least one hour. Shake siphon until sauce comes out smooth and airy.

Fresh hazelnut slices:

Slice the hazelnuts lengthwise using a very sharp mandoline or knife.

Plating:

Place six sea buckthorn berries slightly to the left of the center of a plate.

Siphon warm egg yolk and sea buckthorn sauce on top of the berries until you have a nice round, approximately 8 cm. Cover the round with slices of the fresh hazelnuts.

Place the cooked pumpkin tartlet to the right of the sauce.

Finish with pear vinegar sprays and salt.

Matthew Orlando

AMASS, COPENHAGEN
55.69053° N, 12.61119° E

In a warehouse at an old, abandoned shipyard on the outskirts of Copenhagen, a restaurant with graffiti on its interior walls has quickly become one of the city's hot spots. It's called Amass, it opened in 2013, and it's run by an American from San Diego named Matt Orlando. Having cooked in some of the world's most celebrated kitchens, from Le Bernardin and Per Se to Aureole, Le Manoir aux Quat'Saisons, and Fat Duck, Orlando was ready to run a kitchen all his own. But don't call it New Nordic: Orlando wants his guests to know there's an American in charge. And yet Amass couldn't exist anywhere else but the Danish capital.

Why did you first come to Copenhagen?

I met René [Redzepi], chef of Noma, in 2005 and moved to Copenhagen to work for him for two years. That was also the year I met my wife, who also worked at Noma; we've worked together in the kitchen for 11 years now. A few years later, I left Noma to work at Per Se in New York, but I eventually returned to Copenhagen to be the head chef of Noma—and I'm still based in Copenhagen now.

What was it like working at Noma?

Intense. I learned so much about respecting products; I've really carried that with me. René also has this way of pushing you beyond what you think is possible.

How would you compare Copenhagen to the other cities you've worked in?

Copenhagen is a very special city in which to have a restaurant. The sense of collaboration among restaurants is amazing here. Of course, there's a sense of competition too, but in a very healthy way; everyone supports and promotes each other. Most importantly, everyone shares information.

You've really cooked everywhere. Why open Amass here in Denmark and not anywhere else in the world?

The food we cook at Amass could not exist anywhere else in the world. It's weird to me when you see people with restaurant concepts and menus that can be inserted into any city on earth. Although, Red Hook in Brooklyn was a major inspiration for the way the restaurant looks. When I lived in New York, I spent a lot of time down there. I just loved the post-industrial feeling of those old, abandoned warehouse spaces. Events that used to happen in a space give it residual energy. These kinds of spaces have so much character.

Tell us a little bit about the Amass space.

I loved how open it is. It immediately makes people relax. The ceilings are high. It makes you breathe more. When I first saw the place, every wall was white. It looked sterile and huge. My first reaction was to be excited, followed immediately by, "Oh, shit. How are we going to make this space feel warm and comfortable?" My wife, our friend, and I just sat in the middle of the room with a sketchpad and started thinking of ways to make it work.

What about the graffiti in the interior?

Graffiti has been a big part of my life since I was young. The friends I grew up with did graffiti. One of my skateboarding friends knew the artist SOTEN, who is probably the most famous graffiti artist to come out of Copenhagen. Now he does a new piece for us every year. And every new piece changes the feel of the dining room.

What was the moment you knew you wanted to open a restaurant?

It happened while I was at Per Se. About a year and a half into my three-year contract with Thomas Keller, I called René to ask what was going on in Copenhagen, because I realized that was really the spot where I wanted to open a restaurant. I told him I wanted to come back and work for one year in Copenhagen just to meet the farmers and purveyors, get back into the scene. I didn't want to go back to Noma because I had already been there, and I wanted to do something new. He told me he would put feelers out. Except he called back a week later saying, "This is stupid...you should come back to Noma. I've never had a head chef, and I keep going back and forth with who that should be, but I need to hire and it keeps coming back to you." How could I say no?

How long did you stay?

When I got to Noma, it was total chaos. It took me a year just to get the kitchen in order. There was a huge learning curve, because I had never been a head chef anywhere. Internally, I was thinking: How do I take all of the organizational skills that I've learned working for Thomas Keller and implement them in a way that works with Noma? They're two very different restaurants. Noma has a lot of gray areas, which allow it to evolve and change; with Thomas, it's very much black and white.

How do you run your kitchen here at Amass?

This kitchen is everything that I've loved about the kitchens I've worked in and none of what I hated.

What are some of the things you've liked—and some you've hated?

For one thing, we don't have a test kitchen here. I don't like the concept of the test kitchen. Yesterday, we put three new dishes on the menu, untested. We are so tied to the seasons so, when you get a snowstorm on Saturday night, you get calls the next morning from purveyors who say that artichokes aren't coming in, mushrooms are done, and there's no more watercress. There goes half the menu. But, if you're a chef, you should be able to work with what you have as any craftsman would.

What do you do when the weather changes what's available?

We adjust and rewrite the menu based on what the farmers tell us is still good. We knew there would be carrots, so we built a dish around those, adding in some shaved dried lamb's heart, a fermented vinaigrette, and burnt broccoli. It was the first time we served that dish, but our guests told us, "That's the best dish on the menu." It was stressful, but at the end of the night, I just looked around and thanked the team. We really smashed that day.

You have an insider-outsider perspective. How would you characterize Danish cuisine?

I think it's more about Scandinavian cuisine, in general, than Danish cuisine in particular. Norway, Sweden, and Denmark basically have the same six vegetables to work with in the wintertime.

What about the idea of New Nordic?

New Nordic cuisine doesn't exist. Nordic cuisine, in general, is about using whatever ingredients you have around you. Why this type of cuisine is really popular now is that, for so many years in Scandinavia, everyone has been looking south to France and Italy for inspiration. No one looked here. This way of thinking is so old—regional cooking is not a new concept. But, here, there are so many ingredients just being discovered because no one ever cooked with them. In that sense, it's very exciting to have a grass that tastes like coriander that grows abundantly on a beach that no one has ever cooked with.

How were Danes cooking before this?

In Sweden, they have a cookbook called *The Brown Cookbook*; everything in it is brown. Traditional Scandinavian cuisine is not exciting. It's a Protestant part of the world where pleasure is not something people strive for—and that ethos has carried over to cuisine. Young chefs here don't have the same entrenched reference points to adhere to the way that Italian and French chefs do, where they're afraid to mess with grandma's cassoulet too much. We just don't have those rules here. It's liberating.

How would you characterize your cooking style?

I am very spontaneous. Stereotypical Nordic cuisine is very green and very acidic. When people come to Amass, they often say they can tell an American is in the kitchen, because there are also very strong flavors. We certainly use a lot of vinegars and ferments here, especially in our bread-making.

Do you have any favorite ingredients you like to cook with here?

It depends on the time of year. In the summer, tomatoes are amazing. Right now, we're getting really good plums and shellfish—squid, in particular, is outrageously meaty here.

If you could cook for any chef, dead or alive, who would it be and why?

Once upon a time I worked for two years for a chef in San Diego named Frances Perrot. He was born and raised in Paris, worked for all the big guys when he was young, and then moved to California. To this day—even after working for René, Thomas, and Heston—no chef has had the same kind of impact on me as he has. He taught me what it means to be a chef, about the kinds of sacrifices you make—real life lessons. He created such a strong foundation for me to go out and be confident when you walk into new places. And technical stuff too: I know how to flute a mushroom; how to tournée; how to dice; how to truss a chicken. All of these techniques that are being forgotten because everyone's looking for the hot new, modern way of cooking. I'm so thankful for that foundation, and I'm so thankful for Francis Perrot. I'm just getting goosebumps right now just thinking about cooking for him.

Squid, Egg Yolk, Black Garlic, Plums, and Bitter Radish

Recipe by Matthew Orlando from Amass.

Prep time: 1 day
Cooking time: 1 hour
Assembly: 5 minutes
Serves: 4

Day before serving

Clean squid, taking care to remove all innards and cartilage.

Cut one side length-wise to open the body up. Clean both sides of flesh by rubbing with a damp towel.

Lay squid flat on a tray and freeze overnight to tenderize.

In a small bowl, chop black garlic and place in 50 g of grapeseed oil.

Reserve at room temperature until preparation.

Serving day

Place whole eggs in boiling water for 14 minutes. Shock in ice water to prevent further cooking.

Separate egg yolks from whites.

Place yolks in a high-powered blender with 50 g of water. When purée is smooth, and while the blender is still running, slowly drizzle in 100 g of grapeseed oil. Season with lemon juice and salt to taste.

Strain egg yolk emulsion through a fine-mesh sieve and reserve in refrigerator.

Remove squid from the freezer and cut into small pieces that are approximately 2 ½ cm by 2 ½ cm.

In a medium sauté pan, add 100 g of grapeseed oil and cook squid over high heat for 30 seconds. Drizzle with black garlic oil, a touch of salt, and lemon juice.

Cool in refrigerator.

•••

2	whole squid (approx. 200g each)
6	whole eggs
250 g	grapeseed oil
3	cloves of black garlic
1	large, bitter radish
1	plum
10 g	apple cider vinegar
4	whole calendula flowers
60	whole swamp cress shoots
1	lemon
1	pinch salt

Squid, Egg Yolk, Black Garlic, Plums, and Bitter Radish - *continuation*

Peel and thinly slice bitter radish (using a mandoline or very sharp knife, to approx. ¼ mm slices) into 24 pieces. Season with salt and a few drops of lemon juice.

Place slices in refrigerator for 10 minutes to tenderize.

Remove pits from plums and thinly slice (approx. ¼ mm) into 20 pieces.

Marinate slices in 10 g apple cider vinegar at room temperature.

Plating

Place a teaspoon of the egg yolk emulsion onto the center of each plate.

Distribute the squid evenly among the plates and place over the egg emulsion.

Spoon chopped black garlic evenly over the plates.

Evenly distribute 6 slices of both radish and plums over each plate.

Garnish with swamp cress shoots and calendula petals.

Carrots, Pickled Wild Roses, Sour Curd, and Mustard Shoots

Recipe by Matthew Orlando from Amass.

Prep time: 1 day
Cooking time: 1 hour 20 minutes
Assembly: 5 minutes
Serves: 4

Day before serving

Peel carrots and steam until tender (time will depend upon thickness of carrots). Place in a dehydrator overnight at 40°C. Reserve juice.

Place 100 g of yogurt in a vacuum-sealed bag and steam for 40 minutes in a steam oven.

Remove bag from steamer and let cool in refrigerator.

Place contents of bag into a fine-mesh sieve and let the yogurt drain overnight. This will become your yogurt curd.

Place remaining 100 g of yogurt into a small sauce pot over medium heat, cook until contents appear dry, then reduce to low heat. Stir constantly until solids begin to caramelize.

Remove from heat and place contents in a dehydrator overnight at 60°C.

Remove caramelized yogurt from dehydrator and break into fine crumble.

•••

500 g	carrot juice
200 g	unsalted butter
20	wild rose petals, whole
12	small carrots
5	small pieces elder, ground
3	small nettles
100 g	grapeseed oil
200 g	plain yogurt
500 ml	apple vinegar
18	mustard shoots, whole
1	lemon (for juice)

Serving day

To make pickled rose petals, submerge petals in a bowl of apple vinegar.

In a saucepan, reduce 500 g carrot juice to 200 g and reserve.

In another small saucepan, cook 100 g of butter until the butter solids caramelize into brown butter. Strain off caramelized butter solids and reserve browned butter.

In a small sauce pot, combine 75 g of reduced carrot juice and 75 g of brown butter. Warm over low heat. Season with salt and a few drops of lemon juice. Reserve warm.

Place carrots in a sauté pan with the remaining 125 g of reduced carrot juice. Glaze carrots with juice over low heat.

Place carrots on a tray. Season with salt and sprinkle heavily with the caramelized yogurt crumble.

Plating

Spoon 1 ½ tbsp. carrot juice onto the center of each plate. Place carrots on top of juice and spoon small scoops of the yogurt curd evenly over the top.

Lay pickled rose petals over the top of the curds and carrots. Garnish with mustard shoots.

Purple
Kale

ingredient
glossary

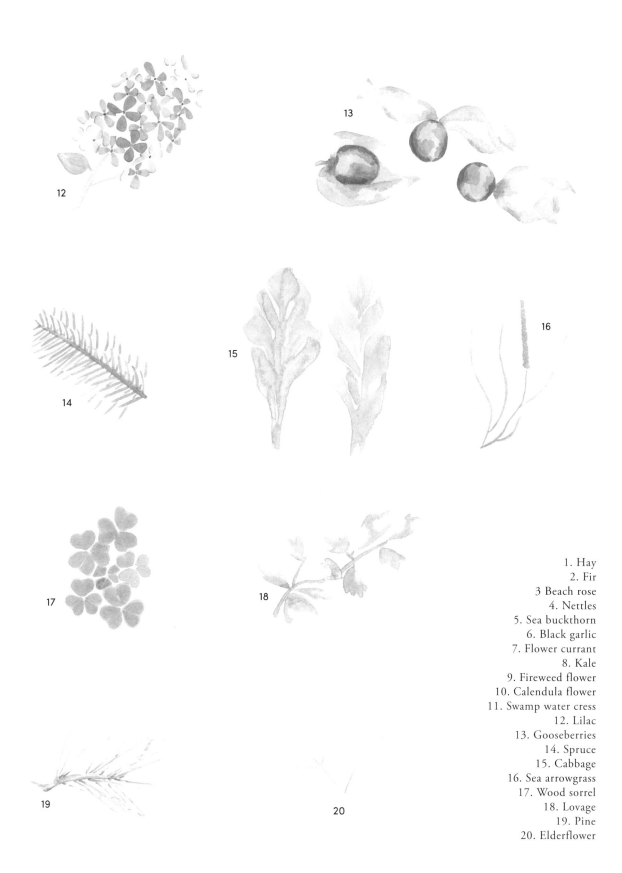

1. Hay
2. Fir
3 Beach rose
4. Nettles
5. Sea buckthorn
6. Black garlic
7. Flower currant
8. Kale
9. Fireweed flower
10. Calendula flower
11. Swamp water cress
12. Lilac
13. Gooseberries
14. Spruce
15. Cabbage
16. Sea arrowgrass
17. Wood sorrel
18. Lovage
19. Pine
20. Elderflower

Schønnemann
By Matt Duckor

Before I sat down to lunch, I honestly thought I might have been in the wrong place.

Maybe it had something to do with the large Danish flags flanking the entryway. Or perhaps it was the pair of heavy-set Danish retirees basking in the endless sunlight that marks summer days in this part of the world. Slurred words from an early schnapps-drinking stint elsewhere poured out from their lips. It's the kind of restaurant I usually walk past without a second thought. I walked in anyway.

Down a set of four steps, I entered a basement dining room. There was no friendly host tasked with keeping an eye out for Michelin inspectors or cadres of chefs prepared to greet diners. Instead, there was just a bartender, checking my name against a tidy, handwritten list and seating our group with little more than a nod.

It was exactly where I wanted to be, at Schønnemann, one of Copenhagen's oldest and most hallowed restaurants. It doesn't have an Instagram account and the chef isn't known by name. Yet the city's current power player chefs, such as Bo Bech and René Redzepi, recommend Schønnemann without reservation. They like it because it's old-school, it's an experience, and because it doesn't preoccupy itself with hype. They also love it because it's damn good.

Since opening in 1887, the restaurant has earned itself a reputation for serving some of the country's finest smørrebrød, the classic, but often poorly executed Danish open-faced sandwich found everywhere from airport kiosks to office cafeterias across Copenhagen. Schønnemann's roster of sandwiches has the power to completely alter the way you think about rye bread. In Denmark, they call it *rugbrød* and it takes the form of squat, dense loaves packed with hearty flavor and the structural integrity to hold up to everything from smoked herring to thin slices of roast beef and shredded fresh horseradish.

Once seated in the restaurant's sun-drenched dining room, there is only one possible course of action: Settle in for a long lunch—the only meal served—and start with the restaurant's best dish: A glistening pile of softly scrambled eggs atop a single slice of that toasted rye bread, draped with a silky-smooth piece of smoked eel, two slices of tomatoes, and a deep green mess of finely minced chives. It's creamy, bright, and clean—the Danish answer to bagels and lox spread at New York's Barney Greengrass, outfitted with the same sense of pomp and nostalgia as that legendary institution.

Like most of Schønnemann's menu, a salad of Greenland shrimps doused in mayo and covered with chopped bits of hardboiled egg isn't radically different from what you would see at other unremarkable restaurants in the Danish capital—it's just the best version you've ever had.

Skip the Carlsburg on draft. (Though, if you arrive early on a sunny day you might be lucky enough to be offered a pint to enjoy outside, maybe alongside the regulars.) Navigating the restaurant's impressive list of over 140 schnapps through flights of small pours is one of the better ways to spend an afternoon in the Danish capital, trumped only by hopping on a bike to wander the city's winding streets.

The restaurant's true power is shown after the last dish is cleared. As I make my way back up the steps, out onto the cobblestone-lined square, I'm stuffed, I'm tipsy, and I wish I could do it all over again. It's why Schønnemann has been around for almost 130 years.

Per Hallundbaek

FALSLED KRO, FUNEN
55.15298° N, 10.148339° E

In central Denmark, two hours away from cosmopolitan Copenhagen, rolling hills and grassy knolls are a way of life. On Funen, the garden island, which also happens to be Denmark's second largest island, a white thatched-roof cottage welcomes visitors and diners to Falsled Kro, an idyllic inn with a world-famous restaurant. Chef Per Hallundbaek captains that ship. He took the reins of Falsled Kro in 2009, and was tasked with balancing the exacting high standards the restaurant was known for, the history of the place (it's where gastronomy *really* started in Denmark), and the emerging fervor for the New Nordic cuisine coming out of the capital. Yet, even though he resolves to maintain the traditions of the beloved institution—with its bottles of big reds, lobster, and caviar—he also challenges them. He pushes on without distraction, and remains uncompromising, even in the face of so much change. It's what has made him one of the most respected chefs in Denmark.

This restaurant has a deep history. What's the background?

Two hundred years ago this place was a smugglers inn. When that shut down in 1969, it was abandoned for two years before being purchased for a restaurant. But it wasn't until 1971, when two visionaries founded Falsled Kro, that it was up and running. They hired a French chef, who brought French cuisine to this remote part of Denmark. It was actually a big catastrophe at the time; people thought the restaurant was mad for serving roasted quails and snails. In 1971, in Denmark, people were accustomed to eating very heavy meats with boiled potatoes.

Were most Danish restaurants serving French food back then?

Until René and those guys, restaurants in Denmark were French.

How do you view the New Nordic movement?

It's been an eye-opener for me, and a very good thing for Scandinavia. We had all of these amazing products we never used. Now, everyone just goes into the forest and collects moss or picks mushrooms and herbs. That doesn't mean I wanted to do the same thing. Everyone was laughing at René at first, including myself. But they just kept going. When I tasted their food for the first time, it blew me away. When you do something for many years, you get conservative. To see what they did in the capital, where there isn't even any forest, was just amazing.

Your restaurant is in the middle of the countryside, surrounded by green vegetation. How has that influenced your cooking?

We have a garden here where we have 1,000 square meters of our own vegetables. In the summertime, we produce about 80 percent of our own vegetables. We pickle a lot of it to save for the wintertime.

You mentioned the influence of the New Nordic movement. What do you think will happen going forward?

I hope that the ethos of it is here to stay. The only problem is that now guests request more diversity in food. They specifically ask for hot food—not just cold food that is pretty.

How do you develop your dishes?

We change the menu eight times a year. There are two things we look for in our dishes. They should taste good, of course. We are also an old-fashioned gourmet place where we use a lot of truffles and caviar, so we work hard to pair wine seamlessly with food throughout the meal. Right now, there is a natural wine revolution in Copenhagen.

What do you mean?

I'm not against natural wines, but here we cannot serve nature wines, because our clients do not want to drink them. They want heavier, full-bodied reds.

Are most of your clients Danish or foreigners?

From May to August, 70 percent of guests are foreigners—mostly Germans, Norwegians, and Americans. Off-season, we receive people from Copenhagen. This place has always been a refuge for famous people, actors, politicians, and other people who need to escape.

How important do you think it is to combine the dining experience with the inn component of the experience?

It's very important, because that's why people come here. If they have a bad breakfast experience, it doesn't matter how good their evening was. Service plays a very big role. We have to read our guests. If a waiter comes over and starts telling a story about the grandmother who crushed the grapes in the wine you're drinking when all you really want is to have a quiet evening as a couple, you will be unhappy. Sometimes, restaurants over-explain things; food should do the talking most of the time unless you're serving foodies who want to hear every last detail.

Are there any disadvantages to being out here?

Being perceived as approachable is one of our biggest challenges. And, as far as press goes, brand new restaurants get reviews. That's what journalists do: They write about new places. Places close, and other places open that are brand new. But we've been here for 45 years and no journalists are coming here.

Have you ever thought about changing your cooking to something more modern to attract more attention? Or, why have you chosen to keep the food traditional?

We like to think of our food as classic in modern form. It's not heavy; it's a lot of vegetables. We use peak ingredients—lobster, caviar, and truffles but also Pyrenees lamb and chicken breast—but prepare it in a lighter way. At the restaurant, you won't see dishes like lamb or chicken with potatoes.

It's important to maintain the heritage of the place. People do not come here expecting to eat what they just had in Copenhagen. They could have stayed in Copenhagen for that. They come here for the truffles. We are also a Nordic restaurant that cooks with vegetables we grow in our backyard garden.

How does local sourcing factor into the dishes?

If you were somehow kidnapped, blindfolded, and fed our dishes, you should feel that you are in this particular part of Denmark. That's why we only use local fish and vegetables. But, when it comes to meat, people always say Denmark has the best lamb and chicken.

But that's actually not true. In Denmark, we don't have free-range chickens. It's not allowed because the government is so afraid of diseases. It's actually a catastrophe here. It costs twice as much to import them from France, but it's worth it. The structure of the meat and flavor are better because the chickens have been running around and using their muscles.

With ingredients like those, you actually have to think and use your brain to make something. Pork here is great though: We have an organic pig farm we love that's just down the road.

You mentioned earlier that diners want substance, not just cold food that looks pretty. Do you think young chefs need to focus more on flavor?

For the last seven years I've been judge of the Chef of the Year awards in Denmark. Last year, the contestants were given a côte de boeuf that should have been roasted on the bone. The chefs were boiling it, putting it in a bag, and throwing it in a sous vide machine. They were fucking fucked. The food looks very beautiful when you cut into it but it comes out chewy with no flavor at all.

I admire the guys at Noma—how they've done what they've done. But sometimes you get a chef who worked at Noma for nine months, who just has it on his resume, and everybody thinks, "Wow, that chef must be amazing." And when you ask about the kind of stuff they've been cooking, you hear about pine needles. Maybe, if you're lucky, they'll tell you about peeling some onions. But they're not really *cooking*.

Why do you think the focus is on how it looks and the technique instead of how it tastes?

The herbs and flowers are very beautiful when plated. Some of them taste amazing. But when you only serve cold food, it's not really dinner. Dinner is having something that should be cooked, roasted, or braised. When I spoke to some of the chefs after the competition, I realized they were out of practice with those techniques because they either have never done it or

haven't done it in a very long time. The problem is that sometimes you go to a restaurant and it's more about the chef than the food. It's about the fucking guy in the white jacket. It's actually what I like about Noma; it's fantastic to see René in the kitchen. In France, you don't get that very often.

Do you think that more chefs should be in the kitchen cooking?

Yes, absolutely. I am in the kitchen. I am cooking leeks. The more time you spend away from the kitchen, the more things change. Kitchens are run by human beings who want to evolve and do their own cooking. I think that's great. We actively talk about our dishes and workshop them. It's why we change our menu so often—usually on Thursdays. But, at the end of the day, the best dish is the one that's best for the guest, no matter who came up with it.

If you could cook for any chef who's ever lived, who would it be?

It would be this revolutionary guy just north of Barcelona named Santi Santimaria. He had a Michelin three-starred restaurant and he was not educated as a chef. He was an engineer and an architect. But his family had this hotel-restaurant. I went there three times. There was nothing in the city. But you would walk in and your nose would tell you: "They're really cooking here." You would see the coolers and all the game on display. He was really, really cooking—just before chefs in San Sebastian started using all the chemicals. He just kept saying everyone should braise. And then he just died at 53 years old. It was opening day at one of his new restaurants and 50 journalists had just left the kitchen as he was explaining a dish. Boom. Finished, over, out.

When he was explaining about cooking in Spanish, I didn't understand shit, but you could see how passionate he was. I was just a chef living in Norway at that point. If I could cook for anyone, it would be him.

Smoked Salmon with Horseradish Crème and Frisée

Recipe by Per Hallundbaek from Falsled Kro.

On Falsled Kro, we have been serving this dish for over 40 years. We get fresh salmon delivered every Thursday, cut them into fillets, sprinkle with sea salt, and leave them in the cooler for 12 hours. We then cold smoke them for 48 to 56 hours over beechwood.

Prep time: 25 minutes
Assembly: 5 minutes
Serves: 4

Cut salmon into thin slices and place them onto plates.

Grate horseradish into the crème.

Sprinkle salt, pepper, lemon zest, and juice into the crème and whip again until it is almost stiff.

Put mixture into a refrigerator for 20 minutes.

Take a teaspoon and put it into hot water, then make small divots on the salmon and place the whipped crème on top.

Decorate the crème with frisée and drizzle olive oil over top.

600 g	cold-smoked salmon (such as Nova lox)
200 ml	heavy cream
3 cm	horseradish root
15 ml	fresh-squeezed lemon juice
1/2	lemon (zest)
1	bunch of yellow frisée
50 ml	olive oil

Crispy Chicken Egg with Hay Cheese, Savoy Cabbage, and Garlic

Recipe by Per Hallundbaek from Falsled Kro.

This is my signature dish. I make it in four different variations: one with truffles, one with smoked eel, one with cèpes carpaccio, and this one with cheese, cabbage, and garlic.

Prep time: 1 day
Cooking time: 2 hours
Assembly: 10 minutes
Serves: 4

Day before serving

Boil water and vinegar. Poach eggs for 4 minutes then put them into ice water for a minimum of 10 minutes to cool.

Take 2 L water and put 2 tbsp. of salt into water. Swirl around. Remove any egg whites hanging from the poached eggs; store in saltwater and refrigerate for the next day.

Serving day

Add flour, egg whites, and panko breadcrumbs into a bowl. Take eggs out of the refrigerator and roll them in mixture until they are completely covered.

Place eggs on a dish towel and bake them at 50°C for 1 hour.

Peel off Savoy cabbage leaves by cutting off stalks down the middle of each leaf. You will need about 20 leaves.

Boil them in salt water for 2 to 3 minutes, then immediately shock in ice water for 3 minutes.

Boil milk, butter, garlic and pinch of salt. Let mixture simmer for 15 minutes, then strain it through a fine-mesh sieve.

Foam warm mixture in a blender. Only take the foam from the top when serving.

In a separate pan, heat cabbage, butter and ground nutmeg over top.

Heat oil at high heat. Take eggs out of the oven. Put egg in pan for 5 seconds, or until golden brown and crispy. Repeat with remaining eggs. Take care so that eggs do not rupture.

To plate, place egg on top of cabbage. Grate cheese over the top, then finish with garlic foam to taste.

4 eggs
2 L water
2 tbsp. salt
300 ml white vinegar
100 g all-purpose flour
100 g panko breadcrumbs
1 egg white
2 L frying oil (such as canola or grapeseed oil)
1 small Savoy cabbage
125 g unsalted butter
20 g ground nutmeg
25 g hay cheese (substitute with aged Parmesan)
500 ml whole milk
1 garlic clove, cut into four pieces

Rasmus Kofoed

GERANIUM, COPENHAGEN
55.70352° N, 12.57211° E

Rasmus Kofoed, the only person to have won all three statues at the Bocuse d'Or is the chef of Geranium, the first Michelin three-starred restaurant in Denmark. But, really, he's a skateboarder at heart. Kofoed is gutsy and intense, energetic yet relaxed. He's a natural leader who's not above being team player in his own kitchen.

Right now, he's looking out over Faelledparken, a park in Copenhagen's Østerbro neighborhood, recalling why he wanted this location to be the site of his restaurant. This is where he used to skateboard, play soccer, and read books in the sun when he was a kid. As he surveys his world from the upper floors of the soccer stadium where Geranium is located, shimmering with memories like Sweden shimmers across the water in the distance, he says, "I just knew we could do something special here."

How would you describe your cooking style?

I've been eating vegetarian food since I was a kid, so that's how I've always cooked at home. For me to give my all in the kitchen, I need to feel good. It's a tough business, so it's important for me to eat healthy.

What about the food at the restaurant?

I like to use seasonal ingredients; it's just more logical. The biodynamic farm that we work with is 40 minutes away and it has the best products I have ever seen. It's also cheaper because I buy directly from the farm. It's important to be inspired— by the season, by the world. I try to interpret nature; I grew up near the forest, and looking at the trees out back makes me feel at ease.

How, if at all, has skateboarding influenced your cooking style?

You feel really free when you are skateboarding. If you're on a ramp or going down a hill, you really feel alive. You're pushing yourself to the limit. And if you're afraid of falling, you're never going to be good. That's the way you learn things and get better. I've always been competitive too. I still skateboard at Roskilde; they have a lot of ramps there. I also still street-skate. I slam a little bit harder now that I'm less flexible. But skateboarding has made me who I am in the kitchen.

You're also a legendary Bocuse d'Or competitor. What's competing for that like?

When you're training for it, it's like getting a doctoral degree in ingredients. If you work with monkfish, you need to know every single thing about the monkfish. I also just love the creativity, and working with a team. I've been a captain on the Danish Culinary Team for six years. We

get really close—we wake up together, cook together. It's a lot of pressure, and a huge adrenaline rush.

What, if anything, from the Bocuse d'Or have you incorporated into your kitchen?

The first time I competed in the Bocuse d'Or, I looked at what former chefs did and thought hard about what the judges might like. But the judges are from all over the world though and it's hard to please an Asian judge, a Finnish judge, and a Mexican judge when you're thinking that way. What really helped me was beginning to trust myself, and use ingredients that I really love and believe in.

How do you see Danish cuisine evolving?

Back in the day, only French chefs were in Danish kitchens. They would fall in love with beautiful blonde Danish girls, move to Denmark, and then open restaurants. But I came up with the very talented generation of chefs like René. I'm in my forties now, and they are all around my age. We were just curious to define Danish gastronomy—look at its past, think about its future, work with local ingredients, and learn from the older generations.

What do you cook at home when you're not in the restaurant?

We always cook vegetables and copious amounts of herbs at home. I love Vietnamese cuisine with its handfuls of fresh mint and big flavors. I also believe that cooking vegetables for my kids and family will make them strong and healthy. If I just fed them meat, it would be difficult for them to learn to love vegetables. But, because I'm starting them with vegetables, my kids will develop a taste for them and, if they want, choose meat later on. We also eat gluten-free at home, even though we're not allergic. Only on Sundays do we buy bread or croissants from Maya at Café Rosa. I can't eat like that every day. It's about finding the balance with food that helps your body perform best.

If you could cook for any chef who has ever lived, who would it be and why?

I've already cooked for him: a Belgian chef named Roger Souvereyns. I worked in Belgium at a really exceptional two-star Michelin restaurant. Even 10 to 12 years ago, it had its own farm and was serving its food on ceramic plates. It was really ahead of its time. Souvereyns was famous for his deep-fried chocolate ganache. I had the privilege of cooking for him once, and it was an emotional experience. He was crying, and it was such an honor for me. He's such an inspiration.

You're often on the road. What are your favorite countries to travel to?

I love Asia. I've been to Thailand five times. Every time I go, I think I'm tired of it, and I say I'll never go back. The next thing I know, I'm on a boat to Phi Phi Island again. Next time, it needs to be Vietnam. I just love the food. But I have a hard time when I think about their ingredients: I feel so bad eating an egg from a caged chicken. I also love San Sebastián. It has everything you need if you're interested in art, food, and history. The third one is the Maldives, because it's where I learned to make the world's best fish stock.

Do you think it's important for a chef to be in the kitchen all the time?

I think it is. Customers are disappointed when they see chefs traveling all the time. Of course head chefs and sous chefs do a great job, but I think it's important to inspire the team and keep everyone motivated; to do that, I think you need to be present in the kitchen.

What role does presentation play in the food at Geranium, which is well known for its plating?

Sometimes, I find dishes too complicated. You don't actually need so many steps and ingredients to make a dish interesting. When I was a head chef at another restaurant, I was always told that my food needed to be crazy. We were cooking lamb testicles, putting goat cheese in desserts, and adding Coca-Cola to desserts. But, as I get older—I've been cooking for 22 years—my cooking is moving closer to what I actually like to eat and what I feel good about presenting on a plate.

What's the craziest thing you ever made?

I like rap music, and I've been to a lot of rap concerts. Once I went to this a concert by an American rapper named The Game. He passed around a joint on stage—telling the audience it was "strong, Danish stuff"—and he got so high he couldn't rap anymore. That was hilarious. So we once served a dish that we injected with Danish hash. It was a lot of fun.

Cabbage in Creamy Rye and Wild Mushrooms with Hay Cheese and Parsley

Recipe by Rasmus Kofoed from Geranium.

Quick, easy, and tasty—this seasonal vegetable dish is favorite at my house.

Prep time: 30 minutes
Cooking time: 30 minutes
Assembly: 10 minutes
Serves: 2

Cook the rye berries in broth until tender, for approximately 30 minutes.

Add grated lemon zest, cheese, parsley, salt, and black pepper to cooked rye berries.

Add olive oil to pan at high heat.

Cook the brussel sprouts and mushrooms until mushrooms are cooked through and tender.

Plating

Mix brussels sprouts and mushrooms into creamy rye berry mixture.

Garnish with chopped parsley or small leafy greens to taste.

100 g	rye berries
300 g	vegetable broth
250 g	brussels sprouts
200 g	wild mushrooms
30 g	Danish hay cheese, grated
1	lemon, zest
3 tbsp.	chopped parsley
1 tbsp.	olive oil
1 tsp	black pepper
1 tsp	salt

Celeriac Baked in Salt with Raw Apples, Pickled Wild Onions, and Hazelnuts

Recipe by Rasmus Kofoed from Geranium.

This is a healthy recipe that I cook for my family during the winter.

Prep time: 30 minutes
Cooking time: 2 hours
Serves: 2

Clean and rinse celeriac. Dry root with a towel then cover with salt.

Bake celeriac root in the oven at 200°C for 2 hours.

Cut apples into small pieces, any shape you wish.

Whisk apple juice, apple cider vinegar, and hazelnut oil together with a touch of salt.

Break through the salt crust and scoop the insides of the celeriac root out with a spoon.

Place a few slices of the insides of the celeriac on a plate.

Sprinkle with the fresh lemon verbena leaves and drizzle the vinaigrette over top.

1	medium-large celeriac root, unpeeled
300 g	salt
1	Elstar apple
1 tbsp.	pickled wild garlic
1 tbsp.	hazelnut oil
1 tbsp.	apple juice
1 tbsp.	aged apple cider vinegar
	lemon verbena to taste

Bo Bech

"Geist is the closest you get to a brothel without having sex," says chef Bo Bech across the table of his Copenhagen restaurant. Opened in 2011, Geist, named for an abbreviation of the Danish word for enthusiasm ("begeistring"), opened with one objective: to make people happy. "It sounds simple and easy, but it's something restaurants fuck up so often. Either we're obsessed with turning a restaurant into a trendy party or we ruin what could be a pleasurable experience with stiff wine and food." Bech, part of the group of young, hungry chefs who put Copenhagen dining on the map, accomplished what he set out to do at Geist, and at his first restaurant Paustian. Now, he has his eyes set on New York.

What role should happiness play in restaurant dining?

We're all getting busier and busier. We're on this treadmill, where even if we're not busy, we make it look like we're busy. We forget to slow down. The word restaurant actually comes from the word restore. In many ways, a restaurant is like a gas station. You should be able to pull up the car, refuel, and feel ready to go.

You closed a Michelin-starred restaurant, Paustian, to open Geist. Can you describe the decision-making process?

Closing Paustian was a really difficult decision. When I was opening that restaurant in 2004, I had no money. I had just spent it all traveling. I needed a loan but couldn't get one. To get that loan, I actually set up a camping stove outside of the bank, went to the bank director, and said, "This is what I would love to do." I needed her to understand. I cooked her a leek dish, she laughed her ass off, and then she finally gave me a loan. We opened up Paustian with basically nothing—six people just killing ourselves at all hours. We got two great reviews almost immediately, and it gave us instant success.

What was Paustian like?

It was white tablecloth—no music, very fancy. There was a lot of space between the tables. It had an open kitchen, which I loved because I could see who I was cooking for; it was very exciting and motivating as a chef. We were having fun in the kitchen, but everything was so stiff, exact, and intimidating for the diners.

How did those reviews influence the early days at Paustian?

It was like a snowball rolling down a mountain. Paustian opened right in the middle of the period of Spanish dominance, when intellectual food was the hot thing. Some people were using that one awful term for that delicious food: molecular gastronomy. I never understood that. But we kept growing and growing and growing. We eventually outgrew the place. Around seven years in, my two partners at Geist came knocking on my door and said that they had a new space for a restaurant and wanted me to cook there. Rather than saying no and closing the debate, I made counter offers, thinking they'd never say yes.

Did they say yes?

They gave me more than I thought I could possibly get. And, during that whole process, I came to the realization that I achieved more with Paustian than I ever thought I would be able to. It was a beautiful part of my life, but it was better to end it on a high note and take the new opportunity.

Do you think there is a place for fine dining in 2016?

Luxury restaurants will never disappear. It's the equivalent of saying, "Is my beard in fashion?" For the 10 years I've had it, it's been in fashion five times and out of fashion six times. Chefs should cook the type of food they're passionate about.

You used to have a TV show in Denmark, **Med kniven for struben***, that was similar to the Food Network's* **Kitchen Nightmares***. How has that influenced your cooking style?*

It influenced me as a restaurateur—how I approach the business side of it. Once you're in the hurricane, it's very difficult to understand where you are. Most people in my business say they're open-minded and ready to change but, when it comes down to it, they aren't ready to hear criticism.

Was there anything that the failing restaurants on the show had in common?
Those restaurants were lying to themselves. Most of the time, restaurant

owners just wanted to open a restaurant for the sake of opening a restaurant. Most of them lacked culinary education and an interest in making something delicious. But then when they open, and the economy tanks, they cut costs and further decrease quality to save money. The short answer would be: This is a profession that is a beautiful craft that requires training. You can't cheat. If you can't build a wood table, you can't build a house.

Where does Geist fall in the New Nordic movement?

For me, Nordic food is about terroir. But we are in the heart of Copenhagen. It's not like we are cooking out of little cottages on the mountainside; we shouldn't make our food look like we're cooking it on a farm when there are cars buzzing by outside. Our guests are international, so I actually like to incorporate a glimpse of foreign ingredients. Each dish is like a little kiss from my travels. When I went to Montreal and saw how maple syrup was made, I introduced it into my food with that memory in mind.

You've cooked in Japan, New York, Mexico—all over the world. How has travel influenced your cooking?

Traveling is so intoxicating. It's reinvigorating. As a chef, you have to make sure you're taking care of yourself because otherwise you'll burn out. Travelling is my way of going out and refueling—not because I need a new idea, but because experiencing those things makes me feel alive.

When you are an experienced traveler, there is this internal challenge of wanting to keep experiencing new things, but also going back to the same sensations you love. To travel is also to be brave. To really travel, you leave security at home—leave behind your common routines, your friends, the things you know. You are going down a road where everything is new to you; I'm in love with that feeling of not knowing. But it can also spark internal conflict if you have a fashionable disease called FOMO (fear of missing out). When you travel, you need to be present.

What's your favorite place to travel for food?

Japan. The Japanese have devoted themselves to the act of being slow, and they're so damn good at it. Each time I leave, I sit on the plane and think about two things. One: I need to pull myself together and start working better. I need to be better. Two: I think I should just quit my profession and that I must be a disgrace to the whole craft. They are so devoted.

You've recently moved to New York, and are hosting a series of pop-up dinners, Bride of the Fox, to generate buzz for a new restaurant there. Why did you choose New York?

The reason I want to do a restaurant there is because I want to expand my own alphabet. The more excited I am about cooking, the more successful I'll be. So I decided to do a road trip around America, and learn more about the heart and soul of American cuisine. What does it mean to eat a lobster roll at Red's Eats in Maine? How does it feel to get barbecue sauce in your beard in Kansas? Does a pizza taste better in Los Angeles than it does in New York? While I was doing that, I realized that it's not New York that needs me; I need New York.

New York is a notoriously difficult city in which to open a restaurant. How is it going so far?

About six months ago, I started studying how other immigrant chefs opened restaurants in New York. I was rather devastated to learn how difficult it was for renowned foreign chefs to come in and think they could teach Manhattanites about food.

First you have to immigrate and get visas. It takes forever. While you're in the process of doing that, you have to find a space. Finding a beautiful space in New York isn't hard; finding one you can afford is. While I was looking, I realized I missed cooking. I had all of these ideas from all of the new produce and flavors I encountered, so I thought, "How can I create a platform where I can cook while I get everything in order without risking going bankrupt?" I turned to the simplest and oldest trick in the book: Throwing a dinner party.

What's your outlook on Danish cuisine in 2016?

Danish cuisine in 2016 is struggling. Denmark is a very open-minded country. We're very curious about what happens beyond our borders. But, because we're very open, Danish food culture is constantly being challenged with rice, pasta, pineapples, lemons—products that don't come from here. On the one hand, there are so many restaurants promoted under the umbrella of New Nordic, which I guess describes clean, light, vegetable-driven, dairy-heavy food. On the other hand, we're not working with our true culture—which would involve incorporating these outside influences. It doesn't make any sense.

What's your process for coming up with new dishes for your restaurants then?

These days, it's very fashionable to say you have a test kitchen and you push stones up mountains. We do it much more organically. If you train yourself just to be open when ideas come, you always arrive at an idea as if it were a letter from God. It happens at the stupidest times—when you're busy, usually—but then you have to go with it. But if you train yourself out of that process—of letting in those spontaneous ideas—you'll be able to access it less and less.

How important is it for a chef to be in the kitchen every day in a restaurant?

At Geist, we serve between 150 and 250 customers a day. It's very important for the chef to be present. Most people tackle the question with the simplicity of, "Oh, it's like man and woman making love. You have to be there physically." When I say present, I mean more that the right heart and soul needs to live within the restaurant. That's how I'm present. I used to be there seven days a week, then six, then five. But there are more than 70 people who work there. If I keep blocking them from rising, I'm failing as a leader.

Langoustine Tartare with Yuzu and Hibiscus

Recipe by Bo Bech from Geist.

Prep time: 1 hour
Assembly: 5 minutes
Serves: 6

Peel and clean langoustines.

Finely cut langoustines into 4 slices.

Roll each slice between two pieces of wax paper so it fits the size of the plate.

Mix heavy cream and yuzu juice, and let stand at room temperature until mixture becomes thick and creamy.

Blend hibiscus flowers into a fine powder and sift through a fine-mesh sieve.

To serve, remove wax paper from each side of langoustines, and present pieces of similar size on a plate. Season with salt.

Add a spoonful of the yuzu cream at the edge of the plate, and sprinkle with hibiscus.

8-10 pieces of Norway lobster

180 g heavy cream

20 g yuzu juice

20 g hibiscus flowers

1 pinch of salt

Black Cabbage with Fried Egg and Wild Garlic Capers

Recipe by Bo Bech from Geist.

Prep time: 15 minutes
Cooking time: 20 minutes
Assembly: 5 minutes
Serves: 4

Wash black cabbage and dry thoroughly.

Swirl cabbage into a loop shape, then chop finely across. Remove the coarsest stems.

Wash fresh sorrel and lay on a towel to dry. Dab with paper, if necessary, to ensure that it is dry.

Take 4 to 5 leaves of the same length and lay one on top of the other. Chop finely with a sharp knife.

Fry the 4 eggs until yolks are runny but whites are set.

Heat butter in a sauté pan at high heat until it gets very hot. Add cabbage. It may take on some light color after a few minutes.

Once butter is sufficiently heated, remove from the heat and add salt and lemon zest. Remove cabbage from pan and set on a piece of absorbent paper (layered paper towels work).

Top the cabbage with chopped sorrel leaves and salt-cured wild garlic capers.

When fried egg is finished, lay in the middle of each plate. Place finished cabbage, sorrel, and wild garlic capers around the yolk.

4	eggs
	salted butter
200 g	black cabbage (cavolo nero)
1	pinh of salt
1	lemon
100 g	fresh sorrel
50 g	salt-cured wild garlic capers

Rocket Launch
By Matt Duckor

For every 50,000 people in Denmark, there is one craft brewery. (For contrast, that number is 170,000 in the United States.) Craft brewing is big business in the Scandinavian country, and much of this boom can be attributed to Mikkeller, the cutting-edge brewery founded by Mikkel Borg Bjergsø out of his home kitchen in 2006. A decade later, you can find Mikkeller beers in over 40 countries, including at Mikkeller-owned bars in San Francisco, Stockholm, and even Bangkok. It's that level of success that has spawned and energized a young group of brewers across Denmark to invent a new guard of beers, establishing Copenhagen as a world-renowned destination for inventive brews.

Among the brightest newcomers is Rocket Brewing Company, founded by entrepreneur Ulrik Lehrskov-Schmidt, chef Kim Agersten, and former Mikkeller brewer Thomas Schon in 2014. The trio leased and converted an abandoned slaughterhouse ("It's actually got everything you need for brewing—easy-to-clean tile floors, big drains, and lots of water pressure," says Lehrskov-Schmidt) about 45 minutes south of Copenhagen. Rocket brews with a ragtag mix of used, new, and retrofitted equipment—or, as the brewery's website would describe it, Rocket is "the world's largest home brewery."

Rocket Brewery sets itself apart by brewing its beers with Brettanomyces—what hip beer kids call "Brett" for short—a naturally-occurring form of wild yeast most commonly used in Belgian sour beers. While Rocket Brewery does make sour beers, it also deploys Brett into IPAs and Pilsners, adding a layer of moldy-funky flavor (in the best way possible).

Ruby cherry sour
Rocket's newest beer is an unfiltered, unpasteurized, and 100 percent bottle-conditioned sour ale that gets triple-fermented for optimal funk. The whole process takes about nine months to complete and results in a dark, red beer packed with intense cherry flavor.

First contact
This farmhouse-style beer is brewed with rye, adding a layer of clove and peppery spice that complements the beer's citrus-y hops.

Zero gravity
This beer will make you wonder why Brett IPAs aren't all that common. The wild yeast eats up all of the sugar present in the fermenting process, leaving you with an extremely dry expression of pure hops.

Attack of the brett zombies
Barley wine is normally an overly sweet affair—the dessert wine of the beer world. This version spends three months in oak barrels while the Brett eats through that sweetness—hence, Brett Zombies—for a dry beer that's different from any barley wine you've ever had.

Rocket Brewing Company beers are available for shipping around the world at www. rocketbrewing.dk.

Rosio Sánchez

HIJA DE SÁNCHEZ, COPENHAGEN
55.68397° N, 12.56928° E

Follow the Corn
Rosio Sánchez of Hija de Sánchez

It's raining, and Rosio Sánchez, former pastry chef of Noma, is taking a breather from her busy taco stand, Hija de Sánchez, at the Torvehallerne market in central Copenhagen. She's a few feet away from it, and can keep an eye on the place, but she's refueling at nearby Coffee Collective. It's a madhouse, and she'll need the boost.

Sánchez opened Hija de Sánchez in 2015 because she just couldn't get a good taco in Copenhagen. Born in Chicago, and of Mexican heritage, Sánchez was craving the flavors she grew up with and was growing increasingly frustrated with the Mexican food in Denmark.

Tacos could be an accessible entry point. "But there aren't any good tortillas in Europe. My main objective was to do a great, very straightforward tortilla that took care with the quality of the corn," she says. "But my first thought was, 'How am I going to do tacos and tortillas in Europe when it probably hasn't happened here for a reason?'" It would come down to the corn.

Hunting for corn was surprisingly labor intensive. She ran tests on dozens of different varieties from all over the world to see which made the ideal tortilla. Some corn had higher water content. Some corn tasted sweeter. Spanish corn tasted different from American corn. Tortillas made from local corn didn't taste the way she wanted. Her frustration grew—until she got an email from Amado Ramírez Leyva of Itanoní, a corn purveyor in Oaxaca, Mexico. "My jaw dropped when I tried that corn," she says. "It was so perfect."

But hauling Mexican corn in bulk across the Atlantic to Scandinavia isn't cheap. Hija de Sánchez has to import tons of it, pay for storage, and grind it to make tortillas. "The whole process is arduous," Sánchez explains. "Labor costs are high,

and then once you actually do all of it, customers want to pay almost nothing for the finished product."

Danes also know little to nothing about tacos. "What's it like serving tacos to people who haven't tried one before? It's people coming up and asking what the pancakes are made from," she jokes. "They'll say, 'What's the flour?' And I'll answer, 'It's corn.' They ask three more times, 'No, no, no, what's the flour?' And I'll say, 'It's still corn.' 'But what flour?!' Until I lose it: 'It's fucking corn, motherfucker!' Now I try to take a deep breath and really appreciate that I get to do this."

It's worth it for the adrenaline rush alone. When the line wraps around the stand, the in-your-face feeling of interacting with guests and sweating all day in a tiny kiosk is thrilling for Sánchez, who was ready to escape the isolation of Noma's pastry test kitchen.

"I'm basically a line cook again, making tacos for eight hours a day in the summer," she says. She's constantly multi-tasking, pouring a glass of tepache (a Mexican fermented pineapple liquor), and plating lengua tacos while she answers non-food-related inquiries from passersby ("Excuse me, where's the bathroom?").

It's a very different type of chaos from Noma. "It's not easy working with people who haven't come from a meticulous place like Noma; I've been learning to get less angry when things aren't up to the standard they should be." Not to mention, she has a fraction of the support staff she used to have and interacts with customers far more than she used to.

But she still gets to hang with the old crew on guest chef days. When she's not turning out the regular menu, chefs from all over the world make cameo appearances at the taco stand and hijack it with a menu of their own for a few hours. Sánchez laments the fact that restaurant culture has become so exclusive; so many restaurants are 40-seaters with advanced tickets that sell out online in seconds. At Hija de Sánchez, anyone can show up and make small talk with René Redzepi or a famous Japanese chef who is in town for a few days. "It makes people happy and it's fun," she says of the program.

It started when she was trying to figure out a backup plan in case anything happened to the Mexican corn shipment; the whole operation hinges on that corn. She called a chef friend of a friend in Spain, who said he'd be happy to help open a line of communication with a corn vendor in Madrid. Unbelievably generous, he was also committed to helping Hija de Sánchez however he could: "He said, 'When you open, my wife and I are going to close our restaurant and come to Copenhagen to give you a hand. We're going to cook with you.' His wife said they'd wash dishes, whatever I needed. It was just so sweet and kind."

Sánchez's only caveat? They could come and help—but they had to make their own tacos, not hers. And so the chef commanding a 30-person Michelin-starred restaurant left his post and started cranking out tacos in Copenhagen with Sánchez. As did Fabian von Hauske from Contra in New York and Lars Williams of Noma, who prepared a taco with grilled roses, fermented beans, and gooseberries. "It was the most complicated taco I've ever seen," jokes Sánchez. "It was such a Noma taco."

When René Redzepi came through, the stand sold a thousand tacos in just over five hours. For many Copenhagen residents, it's one of the cheapest and easiest ways to try food from rockstar chefs whose food is priced out of reach at restaurants with long waiting lists.

Despite the flocks of people she feeds daily, Sánchez wishes she could cook—really cook—for Rick Bayless. When he ate at Noma a few years ago, no one knew who he was except for her. Sánchez was starstruck; she remembered all the times she watched him on TV and drooled over his restaurants Frontera Grill and Topolobampo in Chicago. That meal was one of her favorite moments in the Noma kitchen. She couldn't believe it was really happening.

It was also the night she knew that no matter where she went or what she did afterward, Noma would always leave a mark. Bayless had requested a lighter menu with fewer desserts than usual that night. But Sánchez had already decided: She would find a way for him to try her potato dessert. So, as the table was finishing its desserts, Sánchez was secretly plating a potato dessert that wasn't on the special menu—and trying to hide it from Redzepi.

He saw her, of course, and asked what she was doing. "In that moment," she says, " I just thought 'I don't care what he says; Rick Bayless is going to eat this dessert.' I knew I got caught, but I just didn't care." Instead of scolding her, Redzepi thought about it, and then just said, "I like it." He started plating the dish with her. According to Sánchez, "It was a really defining moment for me."

Years later, she's doing her own thing full-time. She's hunting for brick-and-mortar spaces to give Hija de Sánchez a permanent home. She's taking some time off to develop new recipes and hoping to return with renewed inspiration. She's selling thousands of tortillas to local restaurants that see the new standard for Mexican food in the city. Mostly, though, she's out on her own, doing her thing her way. She can't bring Copenhagen to Chicago, but she can bring a little bit of Chicago to Copenhagen—and create taco culture where it didn't exist before. As she puts it, "Why do tacos in Denmark? Because there aren't any."

Shrimp and Cabbage Taco

Recipe by Rosio Sánchez from Hija de Sánchez.

Prep time: 45 minutes
Cooking time: 10 minutes
Assembly: 5 minutes
Serves: 4

Crema:

For crema, mix buttermilk, crème fraîche, and a pinch of salt. Let rest for 1 night at room temperature.

Salsa macha:

To make *salsa macha*, heat 200 g of grapeseed oil to 100°C, then turn off the fire before adding the dry chiles. Stir for 1 minute, and let mixture cool. Blend on high speed for 30 seconds.

Guacachile:

For *guacachile*, blend avocado, lime juice, raw jalapeno, coriander, onion, and garlic until it forms a smooth, creamy sauce.

Combine with 20 g of grapeseed oil using a hand blender to emulsify. Reserve mixture in a pastry bag.

Cabbage:

Using a mandoline, thinly slice cabbage. Mix sliced cabbage and crema.

Shrimp:

Deep fry fjord shrimp in grapeseed oil at 180°C until cooked through, a few seconds, then transfer to a non-stick pan.

Sauté shrimp and 2 to 3 heads of garlic with 20 g of the *salsa macha*.

Finish by adding cold butter to the pan. Allow butter to bubble a bit before removing from the heat.

Plating:

On a plate, place tortilla, a small pile of the crema-dressed cabbage, *guacachile*, and sautéed shrimp. Finish with slices of avocado.

200 g	white cabbage, sliced
70 g	crème fraîche
70 g	buttermilk
20 g	chile de árbol
220 g	grapeseed oil
15 g	Maldon salt
150 g	avocado
30 g	lime juice
60 g	jalapeño
30 g	coriander
50 g	onion
15 g	garlic
10 g	butter
5 g	lime
50 g	fjord shrimp (substitute with any small, sweet shrimp)
4	corn tortillas

Fresh Cheese Tostada with Black Beans

Recipe by Rosio Sánchez from Hija de Sánchez.

Prep time: 90 min
Cooking time: 1 hour
Assembly: 5 min
Serves: 4

For *crema*, mix buttermilk, crème fraiche, and a pinch of salt. Save in a squeeze bottle.

In a medium-sized pot, cook beans with salt, oil, and coriander stems for 1 hour.

Grill tomatoes, onions and garlic, blend, and set aside.

In a deep pot, fry chopped onion and garlic with pork fat for 3 minutes on medium heat.

Combine grilled salsa with oregano and epazote. Let cook for 8 minutes.

Blend black beans and add them to the previous salsa. Cook for 20 min.

To serve, add 2 tablespoons of bean paste to a corn tostada. Add cabbage, fresh cheese, radishes, and jalapeño slices.

Finish tostada with *guacachile* and cilantro.

40 g	crème fraîche
50 g	buttermilk
60 g	fresh cheese, such as queso fresco
200 g	black beans
2 kl	water
25 g	tomatoes
20 g	onion
15 g	garlic
1 g	oregano
2 g	epazote
10 g	pork fat
20 g	onion, chopped
5 g	garlic, chopped
5 g	salt
30 g	cilantro
5 g	lime
20 g	cabbage, sliced
40 g	guacachile (See: recipe for Shrimp Tacos)
15 g	radish, sliced
10 g	jalapeño, sliced
4	corn tostadas

Frederik Bille Brahe

ATELIER SEPTEMBER, COPENHAGEN
55.68216° N, 12.58298° E

Frederik Bille Brahe looks more like an aloof model roaming the streets of Paris than he does a chef. As in, you'd never know from his sandy blonde hair, blue eyes, lanky build, and boyish charm that the man can really, *really* cook. There's a similar, unexpected appeal to his central Copenhagen cafe Atelier September. There, he's the mastermind behind dishes for which regulars return three or four times a week, dishes that have become Instagrammed all over the world. Because, at Atelier September, an avocado toast *ce n'est pas un* avocado toast. It's art, and Brahe, armed with intense energy and clarity of vision, is the artist.

Tell us a little bit about yourself.

I'm 32 years old, and I grew up in an affluent suburb of Copenhagen. My father was a surgeon and my mother was a nurse. I went to a hippie school, and I never wanted to learn to read or write. It was not because I couldn't. I just experienced a certain complacency. I wanted to be an architect or an archaeologist, but I also knew that wasn't going to happen.

An archaeologist?

My mom's aunt lived in Rome, and she went to the market every day to buy groceries. I remember the smells and the tastes, the simple food, and how important it was to gather at the table. Those memories are ultimately what made me decide I wanted to be a cook.

Once you knew that was what you wanted, what happened?

I started an apprenticeship in Copenhagen at Kong Hans Kælder. After one year there, I quit because I was bullied. Then I moved to London, where I learned about the intersection between performance and cooking, art and food.

When did you go back to Denmark?

I went back just around the time when Noma started up. I wasn't part of that scene at all. Around that time, I lost my love of cooking, actually. I didn't have any mentors I could trust or learn from. I eventually just stopped making food altogether.

What did you do instead?

I built a record label for experimental electronic music. I was looking for another way to make art. But, trying to make music made me realize that I couldn't express exactly what I wanted in that medium. I could do it through cooking.

What did you do once you decided to cook again?

I started from scratch—like, really from scratch. I didn't trust myself anymore. Nobody respects you after you've been out of the kitchen for two years. I started from the bottom, working at an airport hotel restaurant. It was horrible—just bags of frozen vegetables. But I needed the money. The more I slogged through that, the more I realized that I not only was good at cooking, but I had a lot of feelings attached to it, and a vision for what a kitchen should be.

What was that time like for you?

I was in the middle of a life crisis. I stopped making music; I needed a healthier lifestyle. The club scene is very unhealthy: It's alcohol, drugs, and traveling. But I saw that my hero, Alain Passard, had an opening at L'Arpège, so I applied for it. I actually got the job. I couldn't believe it. But then I met a really special lady and totally fell in love with her; we got married, so I didn't go.

What was happening in Copenhagen around that time?

We were undergoing a very important shift in Denmark. In the 1970s, there was this restaurant in Hellerup, where the chef only cooked with regional ingredients. He was tired of bringing in frogs legs and watercress from France. He created this cuisine that was based around vegetables, where the fish and meat were afterthoughts. It was called Saison, and it was one of the most important institutions in Danish dining history. René [Redzepi, chef of Noma] worked there. Everyone worked there for a brief period of time. If you ask René, he would say, "We owe everything to this guy." He was really the one who created Nordic cuisine.

What was working at Saison like?

I worked there for three years, and worked my way up—first to sous chef and eventually to head chef. The chef there, Erwin Lauterbach, became my mentor and is still my father figure in cooking. He was a painter as well, and he just had a beautiful eye for food. He eventually asked me if I wanted do a restaurant here. Of course I said yes. But, Operation Copenhagen, as we called it, had a lot of restrictions. We would only have the front room, and the restaurant could only operate between 7 am and 7 pm. We were also told that we couldn't serve alcohol.

What did you do?

I always wanted my restaurant to be small; I really like taking part in the day-to-day operations. First and foremost, I love to host. I like being in the storm. When you work in fine dining, you never really meet the guests. And fine dining restaurants are like airports: You only go once in awhile. Everyone is stiff. I wanted to create more of a train station or bus station.

What happens in the restaurant equivalent of a bus or train station?

I wanted it to be a place where people could go every day—a place that fits into people's routines. I was inspired by the Rome, Florence, and Milan stations. Or Paris Bar in Berlin, where you get in and you're thinking: Wow, this place contains life.

Where did you start?

The space is full of things I love: I selected everything from the matcha cups to the water. Everything has value. I see this space as a kind of sculpture, where I make choices that shape the room. Nothing is just there. It's not an ordinary cafe in that sense. If the plates break, it's bad, because they all have stories behind them. In that way, I trust my guests with things that are very special to me.

What about that personalization is important to you?

Why should everything in a dining experience be scaled or conformed to a certain standard? We want regulars. There's a social dimension. We have maybe 70 people who come here two or three times a week. Some come every day. We are part of pivotal social moments in these people's lives. We take that responsibility seriously. We want them to be happy so they become as much a part of the place as the plates and the food.

How does the food factor into that?

We serve everyday food. But it's interesting to create an alternative vegetarian option where you don't even think about the fact that it's vegetarian. It's supposed to be sexy.

How did you build the menu then?

Take the avocado sandwich as an example. When we first started out, the menu changed everyday. I was the only one working here; it was crazy. It cost me my marriage, and everything seemed like a failure for a little bit. But, I sat and thought about foods that are universally loved: What do people like to eat? Burgers, hot dogs, takoyaki—they all have an expression of umami. I didn't want to do those things, but I thought maybe I could work with that same flavor.

The rye bread came first. It's healthy and a keystone of the Danish diet. Then avocado because it's healthy and it's actually something you can eat often. I wanted a clean expression, so I went with olive oil, chives, lemon zest, chiles, and fleur de sel. It created an expression of umami without actually being umami.

How important is it that a dish be healthy?

The body is a temple, and you need to be very careful about what you put inside of it. Your body is an accumulation of everything you do in your life, and it's important to have good energy, because we live in a very crazy world where you can be in the middle of a walk down the street and someone starts screaming at you. This morning, I was walking my dog and a lady almost attacked me because my dog wasn't on a leash. She screamed, "You

can't do that, you asshole." And I knew that it wasn't about me and my dog; it was about her and her terrible life. You need to buffer yourself against these things.

You know in Japan, when you eat, you don't eat until you're stuffed, but you eat until you are satisfied. It's quite weird because European people that go to eat in Japan say, "I'm not full" and then go for pizza afterward. But they aren't in touch what what their body actually needs.

You've cooked in Japan before. How has that influenced your cooking?

I have always been very inspired by Japan. The first thing you learn there is that things take a long time. Nothing is quick.

There's also this feeling in Japan that it's important to take time to be extremely precise. You don't take on too much; you just do what you do very carefully. We fill our lives with too many things. One restaurant is not enough; we have to do three or four. And we have to be number one with a six-star review. We need to be famous. We need to be rock stars. Maybe Jiro is famous, but what about the actual best sushi chef in Tokyo? Or the best, let's say, 50? None of them are rich. None of them have big cars. They are all dedicated to their food and their regular customers.

Where does your style fit into Danish cuisine?

In Denmark, at the moment, we are very privileged that we are exposed to chefs like René, Christian Puglisi, and the Kadeau guys. They've made people interested in food here, and they've inspired tourists to come here and eat.

At Atelier September, we have customers in their eighties and kids who are 15; everyone gets the same amount of respect. There's no snobbery. Some people come to Copenhagen and ask where they can get less pretentious food; it's here.

I never try to be Danish. We buy the produce where it's best, and we buy it at the best price. Sometimes that means that if we buy cheese like Comte, piment d'espelette, or fleur de sel, we buy directly

from the market in Paris. It's more expensive to import ingredients like that, but I don't mind paying it.

You've mentioned a dish tasting clean as being very important for your style. Could you explain what it means for a dish to taste clean, and why that's important?

For instance, one of my good friends is an artist and he says, "If you don't have anything to say, just don't say anything." It's the same idea with food. You have an expression; I'm the creator and you're the consumer. If I'm not precise, it's going to seem like I'm wasting your precious time. When I give you something, I want to be able to give it to you without explaining it. It should speak for itself in very precise language: avocado, chives, olive oil, lemon zest. You should be able to understand it. Because of that, I can establish trust and respect. The other part of it is that clean means balancing high acidity with fattiness and bitterness and salt. It cuts like a lightsaber.

What do you cook at home?

The food I prepare for myself is always simple and made from high-quality ingredients. I never buy bad quality food, because I can't eat it. When I fly, I can't eat airplane food, because it feels like I'm being violated. You sit there, eat horrible food, and then you have to sit there for 10 more hours with this food in your stomach. It's terrible.

What is Danish cuisine to you, and how is it changing?

We're basically living in an era of——nationalism—in the [United] States, in Europe, elsewhere.
Recently there was this government discussion about what our cultural values should be. There were questions like: What is the national Danish dish? Who are our canonical writers and painters? What are our values? In 2015, the signature Danish dish was probably pizza, shawarma, or sushi. Traditional Danish food relies on fermenting, pickling, and curing. But the way we eat now is not the way they used to eat. We still eat

herring and salted cod, but our borders are porous. And I miss *really* traditional Danish food, like pork pie. We've forgotten how to pass on those traditional recipes.

That's why René is great; at Noma, they are trying to rediscover the DNA of Denmark. It's a very important task we put on them—and a big responsibility. Noma isn't only playing with food; it's playing with our identity.

"Avokado Mad" (Open-Faced Rye Sandwich with Avocado)

Recipe by Frederik Bille Brahe from Atelier September.

Danish rye bread is everywhere: We have rye for lunch at home or in sandwiches on-the-go, open-faced or closed. But topping rye with avocado is not yet a classic Danish food. This variation happened when a hungry (also: younger) me went looking for something to add on top of a great slice of seedy rye. Avocados were waiting to be sliced, ready to add creaminess to the dark bread. I tested, upgraded, and iterated until this version came out just how I wanted it to be: the right amount of salt and acid to balance the fat of the avocados. This "Avokado Mad" has since become a signature dish at Café Atelier September, a star that has posed countless times for smartphones since its inception.

Prep time: 10 minutes
Assembly: 5 minutes
Serves: 4

Finely chop chives, so they can easily be sprinkled on top of each sandwich during assembly.

Wash lemon.

Slice rye bread.

Divide avocados in halves, lengthwise. Remove stones and carefully spoon out meat using a large spoon. Place avocado halves upside-down on a wooden cutting board. Thinly slice each avocado half approx. 8 to 11 times from top to bottom.

Gently press avocado halves, one at a time, towards the board, so the slices of the half slip and divide into thin fillets.

Carefully slide the side of a sharp knife against the board beneath the center of the avocado, right where the stone was and place the fillets of half an avocado on top of each slice of rye bread. Fan out avocado strips so that they the cover entire rye slice.

Use the pastry brush to evenly spread each open-faced avocado sandwich with olive oil.

Sprinkle with salt, finely chopped chives, Piment d'Espelette, and freshly grated lemon zest.

1	*loaf rye bread with seeds, high-quality*
4	*avocados, ripe (but not overripe)*
20 ml	*extra virgin olive oil to drizzle*
100 g	*small bundle of fresh chives*
1	*large lemon*
10 g	*Piment d'Espelette*
1	*pinch of coarse sea salt (such as Maldon)*

Yogurt Granola with Zucchini, Matcha, and Basil

Recipe by Frederik Bille Brahe from Atelier September.

Yogurt is a classic breakfast in Denmark. For me, yogurt is at its best when it is neither too sour nor too neutral—just creamy and velvety. Toppings add extra pizzazz, but yogurt should be able to stand on its own or with a light drizzle of your favorite honey. At Atelier September, we strain an organic Scandinavian style skyr to get our preferred texture and flavor for our signature yogurt granola with zucchini jam, matcha, and basil. Much of my inspiration in the kitchen comes from my own visual curiosity. Each dish should be as visually pleasing as it is delicious. I want people to be curious and ask: Why is this yogurt green and why does it feature a jam made of vegetables? This yogurt recipe makes for a sweet, fresh, and spicy breakfast bowl or a relatively healthy dessert.

Prep time: 24 hours in advance
Cooking time: 2 hours
Assembly: 10 mins
Serves: 4

Day before serving

Yogurt:

Churn yogurt with a spoon

Cover surface of yogurt container with a clean linen cloth and tie it around using a leash or rubber band.

Place yogurt container upside-down in a big bowl.

Leave to strain in the fridge overnight.

Zucchini jam:

Thinly slice zucchini using a mandoline.

Layer zucchini in a large, flat container and sprinkle with sugar, lime zest, lime juice, finely chopped ginger, and ½ vanilla pod, including seeds and beans.

Cover or seal container and leave it to soak in the fridge over night.

Granola:

Preheat oven to 150°C.

In a large bowl, mix rolled oats, nuts, and seeds.

In a small Dutch oven, mix olive oil, honey, salt, and vanilla. Bring to a soft boil then immediately remove from heat.

Combine the olive oil honey mixture with the nuts and oats mixture, until integrated and completely coated.

Spread granola into a flat, even layer on a lined baking tray.

Bake until golden (about 20 to 30 minutes). Keep an eye on the granola and turn every once in a while with a wooden spoon.

•••

1 kg	organic plain yogurt
1	small tin high-quality matcha powder
1	bunch fresh basil
200 g	zucchini, medium
150 g	sugar
2	limes
10 g	fresh ginger, finely chopped
1/2	vanilla bean
200 ml	rolled oats
200 ml	mixed nuts and seeds (any combination of almonds, hazelnuts, pepitas, sunflower seeds, etc.)
150 ml	honey
12.5 ml	olive oil
1	pinch of coarse sea salt (such as Maldon)

Yogurt Granola with Zucchini, Matcha, and Basil - *continuation*

Serving day

Zucchini jam:

Place marinated zucchini and juice in a large pot. Let simmer on medium-high heat until the zucchini has softened (about 15 to 20 minutes).

Remove zucchini slices from liquid syrup and place in a large jar or container with enough space to pour the syrup in.

Continue to simmer the juice that's left until it has thickened and resembles a viscous syrup.

Pour syrup over zucchini and leave to cool.

For assembly:

Spoon 1 to 2 tbsp. yogurt in the bottom of each serving bowl.

Gently top with 1 tbsp. zucchini jam, a drizzle of zucchini syrup, 1½ tbsp. granola, and basil leaves.

Using a fine-mesh sieve, sprinkle matcha to garnish.

Blocks
By Mads Refslund, as told to Elyssa Goldberg

What I remember of my childhood was that my father was always tired. He worked the night shift, and would wake up in the late afternoon and return around five in the morning. It was my responsibility to pick up the rye bread; I tried to help him out however I could. Our dinners were usually quick and easy, but the best moments—the highlights—entailed making homemade pizza with him. It's how I realized I really loved to cook.

When I was a teenager, I had several odd cooking jobs, including one in a kitchen, where the owner was killed in a freak accident on a safari in Africa, and another where I cooked on a ferry. It wasn't until I was cooking at a hotel, just before the year 2000, that I met René [Redzepi].

We are around the same age, and became friends very quickly. I remember being fascinated by his experiences working at a Michelin-starred restaurant. At the time, I didn't even know what Michelin was. The way he spoke about that restaurant made me want to quit my job and try something new.

We became friendly, worked a few private parties together, and eventually became roommates. After a few years, we were both approached by Claus Meyer, who asked whether we wanted to open a restaurant. We signed on, we called the restaurant Noma, and we were 25 years old.

I didn't stay on very long. René and I had two very different ways of doing things, and I wanted something to call my own. But the restaurant I was working on came upon financial trouble. The main investor went bankrupt after the financial crisis.

I found myself in a dark hole, and I called Claus to talk through what I should be doing with my life. We ended up buying a piece of land together—a two-hectare organic farm where I grew organic vegetables. It was really inspiring for

me. I felt like a phoenix: It was going to take a while, but I was going to start this whole new chapter in my life and open up an organic vegetable-focused chain restaurant. On the farm, I was building the alphabet for it.

While I was on the farm, I was also taking speaking engagements around the world—in Austria, in France. And one of them took me to a food festival in Washington, D.C. It was the first time I had ever been to the United States, so I decided to take a holiday in New York the week before the festival. I thought I'd go to enjoy the vacation, but instead, I unexpectedly fell into a new life.

I went for a sushi dinner at BondST in Manhattan one night, and I forgot to tip. In Denmark, the tip is included with the check. As I was leaving my meal, the waiter chased me down to tell me that I had stiffed him and ask what he had done wrong. I told him that I was very embarrassed, he was a great server, and I would not have done that if I had known. I gave him what must have been a 35 percent tip, and we started talking. I mentioned I was from Denmark, and he replied that I was lucky to be from the country that's home to the best restaurant in the world. The friend I was with chimed in and said that I had been involved at the beginning, and even though I didn't create Noma for what it is today—René is Noma—I put some stones in the wall. The waiter asked if he could contact me about a restaurant project his boss was working on. I said no, because I was planning on opening my own chain in Denmark.

But he asked again, and I just gave him my number, thinking he'd never use it. The waiter passed it along to his boss, and I got a call the next day asking whether I wanted to grab breakfast. We had good chemistry immediately, and he asked whether I'd be interested in doing a tasting for the partners at a new vegetable-driven restaurant called Acme that would soon open on Great Jones Street. In my head, I only wanted to sign on as a consultant.

Somehow, he convinced me to stay on for at least a year as executive chef—not

a consultant. I didn't want to stay any longer than that, because I still wanted to open the chain in Denmark. But I met a girl here, one thing led to another, and one day I realized I had been here for four years.

Cooking in New York versus Copenhagen is very different. For starters, at Acme, I wasn't cooking for a 28-seat restaurant. I was cooking for over 200 people each night. There was loud music playing. And I had to use completely different products. My philosophy is that I should never import, if I can avoid it. Though I quickly realized that it's hard to find celeriac with the tops still on, but cattails, sumac, and melons are easy to come by. Now I have the right vendors and I have people to turn to whose opinions I trust. I'm so happy that I didn't just fly in here and try to conquer the world by doing exactly what I was doing in Denmark.

It's why it's funny to see so many restaurants in New York saying they serve New Nordic cuisine. When I see that, I wonder what New Nordic even means in New York. For me, it will always mean terroir—cooking with what you find in your backyard.

That said, I wouldn't want my restaurants in New York to be called New Nordic. Why would I move to New York to keep being Danish? From day one, I made a promise to myself that I wouldn't be a part of the Danish community [in New York] and I wouldn't limit myself to only Danish friends.

I have since left Acme, but I'm hoping to open a new restaurant in New York soon. It's taken me a while to find a space—I thought I had one a few months ago, but we lost it—but I feel like it'll all come together soon.

When people ask me whether it would have been better if I stayed in Denmark, I don't know what to say. I love building. Cooking still feels that way—constructing something from scratch, one block at a time.

Overthrowing the Dictators
By Bo Bech, as told to Elyssa Goldberg

Every daughter and son grows up looking up to his or her mother and father with total admiration only to say, one day, "You know nothing," and later, once they're long gone, "Wow, they knew everything." That's how we felt about the chefs who came before us, and that's how young chefs who looked up to us as kids will think of us when they're opening their own restaurants. It's the circle of life.

In the 1960s, 1970s, and 1980s, nothing really happened in the food scene in Denmark. We didn't think our culture was rich, diverse, or interesting. Danish restaurant investors only valued classical French cuisine, which they believed to be the hallmark of fine dining. So, French chefs, who only thought French food was worth serving, were flown in so they could run Danish restaurants. And they demanded quail farms for the mandatory quail eggs and oyster farms for oysters.

By the 1990s, it was like there were four or five chef dictators in control. It was a very difficult period for young cooks who wanted to learn. There were no opportunities for them to advance. The only advice we got was that, if we wanted to move up the ladder, we had to travel. So the talented cooks went to France, Italy, Spain, Germany, and England. Except, no one in Denmark expected that we'd come back.

When we did, the head chef dictators had become so old they weren't working in the kitchen anymore. Restaurants are a young man's game, and suddenly there was this glut of very talented young cooks who had something to offer.

We were invited to these quiet meetings, where the dictators said, "We need someone to run our restaurants." As soon as we agreed, we were taught everything, all their secrets. And when those chefs were ready to step down, we were equipped with the right energy and information in the right place at the right time. It also helped that we had been running these kitchens anyway, secretly.

I remember the breakthrough: 2003. The head chef at Kommandanten, a Danish guy, opened his own restaurant, and it wasn't a French restaurant. We have a saying in Denmark: because the bumblebee doesn't know it can't fly, it flies. Because no one had told him he couldn't, he just did it. And others soon followed.

Chefs stopped thinking about the press. They took risks. They showed their hearts without any walls. I won't say that the rest is history, but everything just evolved quickly from there. Instead of young cooks visiting France, Spain, and Italy to understand food, they now come to Scandinavia. But it must not continue this way, like a runaway train.

I love Nordic cuisine, but I also see it as restrictive. If I love pineapple, I want to use pineapple in a dish. I do believe that parsnips and carrots taste better in northern Denmark than they do in America. But I also believe that people who have seen all of the press about the success of New Nordic cuisine won't think outside of that framework.

There will always be people who are not willing to put in the work, so as soon as they see someone is onto something, like New Nordic, that brings them success, they'll just copy and paste it. Chefs should have their own point of view.

The Nordic way of life isn't the only way, and ours is not the only way to cook. Different cuisines brought to Copenhagen by foreigners should cross-pollinate. Our food should reflect the diversity of our city. If there's a Japanese guy who falls in love with a Danish woman and stays in Copenhagen, he should think of opening a ramen shop, instead of a cookie-cutter New Nordic restaurant. Eventually, everyone will have told the New Nordic story, and it will get boring. Nobody will want to listen.

The city needs more accessible food beyond hot dogs. In Copenhagen, there are so many culinary gaps that must still be filled. It's the only way the city will grow. The alternative is the same as traveling to Las Vegas and putting every token on red.

We are the dictators now, but we should not rule forever.

addresses and coordinates

Amass Restaurant
Refshalevej 153, 1432
København, Denmark
55.69053° N, 12.61119° E

Atelier September
Gothersgade 30, 1123
København K, Denmark
55.68216° N, 12.58298° E

Falsled Kro
Assensvej 513, Assensvej, 5642
Millinge, Denmark
55.15298° N, 10.14834° E

Geist
Kongens Nytorv 8, 1050
København K, Denmark
55.68129° N, 12.58630° E

Geranium
Per Henrik Lings Allé 4, 2100
København Ø, Denmark
55.70353° N, 12.57207° E

Hija de Sánchez
Frederiksborggade 21, 1360
København K, Denmark
55.68397° N, 12.56928° E

Kadeau
Wildersgade 10B, 1408
København K, Denmark
55.67229° N, 12.58897° E

Noma
Strandgade 93, 1401
København K, Denmark
55.67789° N, 12.59629° E

Relæ
Jægersborggade 41, 2200
København, Denmark
55.69302° N, 12.54329° E

Sortebro Kro
Sejerskovvej 20b, 5260
Odense S, Denmark
55.36685° N, 10.38388° E

www.ambrosiamag.com
•
instagram/ambrosiamagazine
twitter/ambrosiamag
facebook/ambrosiamag